# Conversations with Leon

Literary Conversations Series

*Peggy Whitman Prenshaw*
*General Editor*

Photo courtesy Marianne Forrest

# Conversations with Leon Forrest

*Edited by*
*Dana A. Williams*

2/09
University Press of Mississippi
Jackson

## Books by Leon Forrest

*There Is a Tree More Ancient than Eden*. New York: Random House, 1973; Chicago:
  Another Chicago P, 1988.
*The Bloodworth Orphans*. New York: Random House, 1977; Chicago: Another Chicago P,
  1988.
*Two Wings to Veil My Face*. New York: Random House, 1984; Chicago: Another Chicago P,
  1988.
*Divine Days*. Chicago: Another Chicago P, 1992; New York: W. W. Norton, 1993, 1995.
*Relocations of the Spirit: Collected Essays*. Mt. Kisco, N.Y.: Asphodel P, 1994;
  reprinted in paperback as *The Furious Voice of Freedom: Essays on Life*.
*Meteor in the Madhouse*. Evanston, Ill.: Triquarterly Books (Northwestern UP), 2001.

www.upress.state.ms.us

The University Press of Mississippi is a member of the Association of American
University Presses.

First edition 2007
∞
Library of Congress Cataloging-in-Publication Data

Conversations with Leon Forrest / edited by Dana A. Williams.
    p. cm. — (Literary conversations series)
    Includes index.
    ISBN-13: 978-1-57806-989-7 (cloth : alk. paper)
    ISBN-10: 1-57806-989-0 (cloth : alk. paper)
    ISBN-13: 978-1-57806-990-3 (pbk. : alk. paper)
    ISBN-10: 1-57806-990-4 (pbk. : alk. paper)
  1. Forrest, Leon—Interviews. 2. Authors, American—20th century—Interviews.
3. African American authors—Interviews. I. Williams, Dana A., 1972–
    PS3556.O738Z65   2007
    813′.54—dc22                                                    2007009015
    [B]

British Library Cataloging-in-Publication Data available

# Contents

# Introduction

In the foreword to the reissued edition of Leon Forrest's *Two Wings to Veil My Face* (1984), Toni Morrison, after noting that she always knew that Leon Forrest was an author whose books she would choose to keep if she had to reduce her library to five hundred, writes: "Brooding, hilarious, acerbic and profoundly valued life has no more astute observer than Leon Forrest" (xi). The interviews collected here help shine light on this truth, which Morrison came to learn firsthand as the editor of his first three novels. Though he was far too modest to ever admit his genius, Forrest, as revealed both in his novels and in these interviews, was indeed among America's most perceptive and inventive writers.

From his first novel, *There Is a Tree More Ancient than Eden* (1973), to his last, *Meteor in the Madhouse* (2001), Forrest created characters who told stories—stories of agony and of triumph, stories of life and death, and stories of tragedy and comedy. As naturally gifted at telling stories orally as he was at telling them in novels, Forrest made for an ideal artist to interview. His humorous and affable nature as a human being reveals itself in many of the interviews, as interviewers often included "Laughter" in parentheses to highlight the comedic nature of their conversations. So engaging was Forrest as a person, on occasion, the interviewer would promise to ask one final question only to be prompted to ask yet another. His responses are consistently full and detailed; and, he goes to great lengths to explain exactly what he means and to give examples that enhance and develop his points. The candor and clarity with which he responds to the questions he is asked are ultimately what makes reading his interviews such a valuable and interesting undertaking.

Like most literary interviews, Forrest's interviews expand the vision he articulates in his fiction and are, thus, useful points of entry and useful reference points for reading his novels and for understanding his aesthetics. His collection of essays, *The Furious Voice for Freedom: Essays on Life* (1994), is similarly useful in providing another means of access to his artistic vision, but the interviews, because of the question and answer format, provide scholars with both specific responses to the most frequently asked and the most obscure questions alike. In other words, while *The Furious Voice* enables scholars to identify the cultural and literary tradition Forrest creates for himself through his essays, the spontaneity of the interview as genre reduces the filter of produced responses, if only slightly, and allows readers to move beyond Forrest as novelist exclusively and on to Forrest as reader, as teacher, as cultural critic, and as thinker—even as each of these roles informs his role as writer.

Throughout the interviews, Forrest gives his ideas about writing, both his own and writing in general. In terms of a routine, he tells Eugene Redmond that he prefers to write in the morning for as long as he can, to stop and do something else, to continue writing if he still has the energy, and to read in the evening. For Forrest, a good day of writing amounts to three to four hours of intense writing. Interestingly, he claims that writing is not fun for him, at least in part because it takes so much energy and concentration. He frequently notes how he writes a scene over and over again, leaves it for weeks at a time, and comes back to it once he has a "certain kind of coldness" or "toughmindedness" about it. The skill he refers to most often when talking about writing as a task is the art of rewriting, which he sees as the writer's greatest challenge and his greatest reward. On at least two occasions, he tells the story of Dylan Thomas's tendency to rewrite long poems by hand each time he made a change. He likens this obsession of Thomas's to his own obsession with rewriting, which he contends gives him inspiration.

In addition to being committed to the "hard work and discipline" of rewriting, writers, Forrest suggests in a number of the interviews, should, at the very least, be inventive with style, be willing and inclined to raise moral questions, have large ambition, and seek to outdo the masters. When Maria Mootry asks him if there is a message in his style, he responds in the affirmative, noting that a writer who attempts to approach his materials in an imaginative manner will likely be inventive about style and about the mode in which he casts his materials. Without doing so directly, he then posits himself in the tradition of those writers who have, indeed, been "master stylists"— among them James Joyce, Marcel Proust, Mark Twain, Nathaniel Hawthorne, Herman Melville, William Faulkner, Ralph Ellison, and Toni Morrison. These are but a few of the writers Forrest mentions as fellow writers he finds himself seeking to outdo. At various points, he acknowledges the influence writers from varied ethnic and cultural traditions and genres have had upon his quest to write the great American novel, and he similarly and openly acknowledges his admiration of these writers.

When he speaks of his early desires to be a poet, in addition to citing consistently his love, in his early twenties, of Dylan Thomas's poetry, he cites Paul Laurence Dunbar, James Weldon Johnson, Langston Hughes, and Sterling Brown as literary mentors whose ability to transform orality into the written word informs his prose. He also notes his admiration for Rita Dove and Robert Hayden as contemporary poets he is interested in. In terms of playwrights—he admits to wanting to be a playwright at one time before he realized that he was too much of a "snob" to work in theatre—he frequently cites Eugene O'Neill and Tennessee Williams as dramatists he admired, O'Neill particularly for his talents with dialogue. Alternatively, when Forrest sought inspiration for writing monologues, he turned most often to Ellison, Faulkner, and Fyodor Dostoevski. Ultimately, what the interviews reveal is that he admired different writers for their different gifts—Dostoevski for his ability to deal with the soul in agony; James Baldwin for his essays and his willingness to grapple with religion; Ellison for his humor; Joyce and Latin American writers like Gabriel García Márquez for their use of Catholicism in their novels; and Melville, Faulkner, Ellison for their attempt to reconstruct the folk preacher. But as he tells Kenneth Warren, he does more than approach these figures as icons: "The first expression is reverence. . . . The second is to think about, 'Now, how can I cut my own path around this lion or lioness, or conversely, take him or her on in areas that they didn't know that well, but only suggested?'" In yet another interview, he cites this relationship as something other than an "anxiety of influence" but more closely akin to Ellison's notion of "antagonistic cooperation." Even as one inevitably hears traces of Ellison and Faulkner in Forrest's solos, they fight to establish their own positions and to create their own sounds.

Music is in fact one of the greatest influences on Forrest's writing. He tells Mootry that music shaped his consciousness and showed him new possibilities of form and style. He was exposed to music early on in life, as both his mother and his father were seriously interested in black musical traditions. Parental influence also accounts for his interest in religion and spirituality as a major theme in his writing. The complexity of his own religious background—his father was a Mississippi Protestant who sang in and directed gospel choirs, and his mother was a Louisiana Catholic—reveals itself throughout his fiction. As he tells Warren, he was influenced by the ritual of the Catholic church, while his father's Protestant background exposed him to the spirituals, gospel music, and the folk preacher. And it is the folk preacher, he mentions time and again, who, as the bard of the race, gave him "the voice into the conscience of the race" and who, correspondingly, "saved [his] artistic life." Thus, he consistently credits his exposure to both religions, rather than to one or the other, as sources of inspiration for his writing. Similarly, he recognizes his openness to a variety of traditions as a tendency that both alienates him from many of his contemporaries, who sought to disclaim all things non-black, and frees him to use anything he deems useful in his writing.

While his writing does, indeed, reveal his awareness of a wide variety of world traditions and a corresponding willingness to invoke these traditions in his own writing to highlight the complexity of the African American experience, his interviews make these sources explicit. His willingness to admit how heavily he has been influenced by other traditions—he tells Redmond: "I'll steal anything I can get my hands on, man, because everything's been stolen from us"—also helps articulate his idea of how the writer can go about developing his or her imaginative mind, by reading constantly and nourishing oneself upon varied sources and traditions. Notably, it is this unwillingness to borrow from other traditions that he sees as a signal limitation of the Black Aesthetic. And even as he notes on a number of occasions that he does not see himself in the Black Arts Movement tradition, he is clearly aware of the space the Black Arts Movement created for him and for other writers. He tells Charles Rowell: "I don't ever downgrade . . . the energies that were broken open by the political forces [of the Black Power and its corresponding Black Arts Movement], even some that I don't necessarily agree with in the society, because that forced the establishment to look to a middle ground, and that's where my work is. It's black and it's evolved in classical connection."

That his work is as heavily influenced by non-black traditions as it is by distinctly black cultural traditions does not, however, remove Forrest from "schools" of black writing. He sees himself as a part of a tradition of black writers, in fact; among them, he suggests in various interviews, are fellow "club-members" James Alan McPherson, Toni Morrison, Albert Murray, John Edgar Wideman, Robert Hayden, Gayl Jones, and August Wilson. As Forrest frequently points out, one of the ways he removed himself from the characteristic anger of the '60s and moved toward a "coming consciousness" that characterizes these writers was through his experience as a journalist at local Chicago weeklies and then at *Muhammad Speaks*. In the Mootry interview,

Forrest notes that he "could absorb the surface protest of [his] firelight there at the newspapers," which freed him to "seek out the soul of black folk, at a deeper level for the soul-meat of [his] fiction." In this way, he was able to avoid the "one-dimensional heat" that might have otherwise kept him from exploring the complexity of the black experience.

In his first interview with John Cawelti, Forrest reveals his recognition of characterization as the convention through which he can achieve this exploration of complexity. He also acknowledges his penchant for creating complex characters as a way for his writing to add to the body of contemporary literature. In other words, in his quest to "outdo" the masters, he acknowledges a need to go beyond where they have gone or to a place where they have not gone well at all. He suggests to Cawelti, for instance, that he saw how "[m]ost black writing and white writing about black characters [was] limited." Thus, he set out to create fully developed characters who were as *complex* as characters as (if not more complex than) they were *important* symbolically. He similarly recognized a void in the literature, excepting perhaps with Baldwin, where religious and spiritual experiences were central concerns. It is perhaps this interest in religion and spirituality (and, in similar ways, myth) that compelled Forrest to find ways to gain control over chaos. Arguing that America is a nation of chaos, he contends that one of the roles of the artist is to recognize this chaos and turn it into art. The artist's ability to do so, then, "is absolutely essential; you will die as an artist or as a man or a woman," he tells Cawelti, "if you can't do that. . . All the great artists who killed themselves did so because ultimately they couldn't do it." Thus, he uses his novels to transform America's chaos, particularly as it relates to African Americans, into art to save both himself and the contemporary reader.

In true Forrest style, his first novel, *There Is a Tree More Ancient than Eden*, uses religious and spiritual motifs to explore the agony of the contemporary African American as he struggles to come to terms with both his personal and his representative (communal) strife. Throughout the interviews, Forrest notes the influence Morrison, as his editor, had on the structure of the novel and, ultimately, on getting the novel published. It was at Morrison's prompting, for instance, that he added the "Lives" section of the novel. In order to sell the book to her fellow editors and to make the book less difficult to understand, she suggested that he add to his draft a section (which ultimately became chapter one) that introduced each of the characters of the novel and that hinted at their relationship to each other and to the world. It was also Morrison who suggested the title for the novel. Before they settled on

"There Is a Tree More Ancient than Eden," they had been calling the novel "Of Eden and Thebes." He claims he sent her 40 titles in one weekend; and they finally decided on "There Is a Tree More Ancient than Eden" because it "seemed close to a Negro Spiritual" and because it implied some African themes. In addition to the structure and title, Morrison suggested that the "Vision" section be set in a different typeface. Forrest's most frequent comment about Morrison as editor, notably, is that she was an excellent line editor, as she was "very much caught up in language."

When *There Is a Tree More Ancient than Eden* was republished, he added two sections to the novel—Sweetie Reed's letter to President Lyndon Johnson and Pompey Brown's sermon on Martin Luther King, Jr. In the interview on the novel with Cawelti, Forrest notes the connection between the "Lives" section, which ends with commentary on Abraham Lincoln, and "Transformations," the section he added later. Both sections, he argues, are about leadership and its destruction, and "the destruction and resurrection of leaders is also summed up at the end of the 'Vision' section." In terms of style, the novel is by far his most experimental and his most poetic. He tells Rowell that what he was trying to do with the novel was "work with poetry . . . the epic form."

By his second novel, he begins to shift a bit from the poetic form to the more conventional form of the novel. "Almost as an answer to the critics of *There Is a Tree*," in *The Bloodworth Orphans* (1977), Forrest sought to "create a novel filled with characters and a lot of character development," as he points out to Cawelti. And since he wanted to do something with families, he focused on genesis issues and the patterns of orphans. It is also in this novel that we see that influence of his new life as a university professor (he joined the faculty at Northwestern in 1973). He began to integrate ideas from texts he was teaching into his own writing. Because he was teaching things about the oral tradition in Ellison and Faulkner and trying to find connections between African American and Native American literatures, he began to read and to think about these things critically. All of this resulted in his imagination being heavily influenced by myth and orality. His task then became to find new ways to interpret and present ideas that had been present in the culture and in the literature all along.

Because he had succeeded with *The Bloodworth Orphans* in writing a novel "chock full of characters," he felt comfortable focusing on the life of one particular character in his third novel, *Two Wings to Veil My Face*. He returns to the theme of genesis or beginnings in *Two Wings*, as the novel reaches back into the heritage of slavery to show continuities that exist between slavery (the African American Genesis Saga, as he terms it) and the contemporary moment. And then in *Divine Days* (1992), because of its length, he is able to create "the broadest kind of landscape," full of stories, characters, and voices. Fascinated by the ways Joyce "cracked open the novel form with *Ulysses*," Forrest reveals to Rowell that he set out to create a novel that was layered with complexity and that allowed him to capture the vernacular and the cultural nuances of the contemporary African American. One of the ways he achieves this is by invoking jazz as a way of ordering the structure of the novel. Unlike the novels in the trilogy, which have a religious base, *Divine Days* is foremost informed by storytelling, humor, and comedy. And he continues this focus on storytelling, humor, and comedy in his final novel *Meteor in the Madhouse*, at least part of which consists of pages he cut from *Divine Days* (the original draft was 1829 pages, while the final was 1135). As *Meteor in the Madhouse* was published posthumously, there are no published interviews about the novellas that make up the novel. He does allude to *Meteor*, however, in a number of interviews as one of the two projects he was working on after he completed *Divine Days* (the other is a collection of essays reprinted as *The Furious Voice for Freedom*).

I have long wanted to see all of Forrest's interviews collected in one place, if for no other reason than to make them readily available to a growing population of Forrest readers. Thus, I am grateful for the University Press of Mississippi's Literary Conversations Series. In so many ways, the interviews make the novels more complex (by explaining their many layers), while simultaneously making them simpler (by explaining their nuances, thus making them more accessible). The arrangement of the interviews is chronological, based on the dates the interviews were conducted. It was a relatively simple task selecting the interviews included here, as too few interviews with Forrest have been transcribed and published. That there are so few published interviews with Forrest is, after all, ironic as it is clear that he made himself readily accessible to students and scholars alike for general conversation about his own writing and about the literature he taught, read, and loved. Among his papers, for example, are notes from students thanking him for hours of conversation he had with them and for his commitment to their achievement. Similarly, there are correspondences between him and other writers who saw him not only as a great writer but as a friend.

With the exception of the McQuade interview, which she edited to read as a first person account, the interviews included here are in a standard question and answer format. The range of subjects addressed in the interviews is extensive (from familial influences to critiques of literary traditions), and, naturally, there is an inherent degree of repetition; but almost without fail, he expounds upon a point he has made previously in his subsequent responses. Thus, to ensure the greatest benefit to scholars, I have left the interviews unedited.

I am greatly indebted to many people whose encouragement and abilities helped make this book possible. For his encouragement for this collection in particular, I thank Dolan Hubbard; for their encouragement of my ever-growing interests in Forrest studies, I thank Marianne Duncan Forrest, John G. Cawelti, Merle Drown, T. J. and Lois Anderson, Sandra L. Richards, Toni Morrison, and Eleanor W. Traylor. For her invaluable assistance with technical and production aspects of this collection, I must thank Tabitha N. Smith, a budding Henry Dumas scholar in her own right. I must also thank Courtney George, who initially retrieved the interviews for me some years ago as I worked on *"In the Light of Likeness—Transformed": The Literary Art of Leon Forrest* and who meticulously compared Forrest's comments in the interviews with his comments in *The Furious Voice for Freedom* and with selections from his notes, letters, and lectures found in his unpublished papers. I am grateful to the library staff at Northwestern University in Evanston, Illinois, for their willingness to facilitate all my requests with regard to Forrest's papers. I am similarly grateful for the tremendous support I have received from the graduate school and the Office of the Provost at Howard University (and its corresponding Office of Research Administration for administering the Provost's generous grants and awards). So much of my work would be tremendously delayed without Howard's commitment to research and excellence in both teaching and scholarship.

I must thank the University Press of Mississippi for its commitment to Forrest studies; each of the interviewers who responded so promptly with both permission to reprint the interviews and with a Forrest anecdote; and Michael S. Harper for such kind reception. I was not fortunate enough to meet Leon Forrest, but I am convinced of his goodness because of the kindness I receive simply by mentioning his name.

Finally, as always, I thank my family and my friends for inspiring and sustaining me.

**DAW**

# Chronology

1937     Leon Forrest is born January 8, 1937 in Chicago, Illinois. He is the only child of Adeline Green Forrest and Leon Forrest, Sr.

1942–50     Attends Wendell Phillips grade school and wins the American Legion Award as the best male student in his class. Attends Hyde Park High School, where he begins to show promise as a creative writing student and eventually serves as president of the school's creative writing class. Attends Wilson Junior College in Chicago. Attends Roosevelt University. Enrolls in a playwriting course at the extension division of University of Chicago. Drops out of college. Drafted into the army and eventually becomes a Public Information Specialist while stationed in Gelnhausen, Germany. Among his duties is writing feature stories for the 3rd Armoured Division Newspaper, *Spearhead*. Takes classes at the University of Chicago.

1964     Begins writing *There Is a Tree More Ancient than Eden*. Writes for and edits local weekly papers the *Woodlawn Booster* and the *Englewood Bulletin*.

1966     Publishes "That's Your Little Red Wagon," which becomes a part of *There Is a Tree More Ancient than Eden*, in the short-lived magazine, *Blackbird*. Also publishes "Ezekiel, Notes Towards a Suicide; Poem" in the June issue of *Negro Digest*.

1967     *Theatre of the Soul*, Forrest's three-act play, is performed at Parkway Community House in Chicago in November.

1969–73     Serves as an associate editor at *Muhammad Speaks*. Promoted to managing editor in 1972.

1971     Marries Marianne Duncan. Completes an early draft of his first novel and sends it to Toni Morrison at Random House. Meets with Morrison in October and gets a contract from Random House for the novel in November.

1972     Meets Ralph Ellison while interviewing the author for *Muhammad Speaks*. Gives Ellison a copy of the bound galleys for *There Is a Tree More Ancient than Eden*. Ellison later reads his endorsement of the novel to Morrison over the telephone.

1973     *There Is a Tree More Ancient than Eden* is published in May with Ellison's endorsement appearing as the foreword of the novel. Forrest joins the faculty of Northwestern University in Evanston, Illinois, in September as an untenured associate professor.

1977     Publishes his second novel, *The Bloodworth Orphans*, which is also published at Random House under Morrison's editorship.

1978     Advanced to tenure at Northwestern. *Recreation*, Forrest's verse-play, is performed in Chicago in June. *Recreation* becomes Forrest's first collaboration with composer T. J. Anderson and sculptor/painter Richard Hunt.

1982     The opera, *Soldier Boy, Soldier*, is produced at the University of Indiana at Bloomington in October–November. Forrest wrote the libretto for *Soldier Boy, Soldier*, and T. J. Anderson set it to music.

1984     Forrest's third novel, *Two Wings to Veil My Face*, is published at Random House under Morrison's editorship. It is the last of Forrest's novels that Morrison edits. The novel wins the DuSable Museum's Certificate of Merit and Achievement in Fiction, the Carl Sandburg Award, the Friends of Literature Prize, and the Society of Midland Authors Award for fiction. Forrest is also promoted to full professor in the spring semester. He begins to compose *Divine Days*. *Black American Literature Forum* publishes "Richard Hunt's Jacob's Ladder," a tribute poem Forrest writes in honor of Hunt's work.

1985     April 14, 1985 is declared Leon Forrest Day by proclamation of Chicago's Mayor Harold Washington.

1985–94  Serves as chair of the African American studies program at Northwestern, which he had been instrumental in establishing.

1988     All three of Forrest's novels are released in paperback by Another Chicago Press. Morrison writes the foreword for the reissued *Two Wings to Veil My Face*.

1991     Completes *Divine Days*.

1992    Another Chicago Press releases *Divine Days*. The novel wins the *Chicago Sun-Times* Book of the Year Award for the best local fiction of 1992.

1993    The Spring 1993 issue of *Callaloo* devotes a section to Forrest. Forrest undergoes surgery for colon cancer in May. W. W. Norton and Another Chicago Press collaborate to release *Divine Days* in hardback in July (a fire in December of 1992 had destroyed the few remaining copies of the novel housed at Another Chicago Press).

1994    Publishes a collection of essays, *Relocations of the Spirit: Collected Essays*, with Moyer Bell. The collection is reprinted in paperback as *The Furious Voice for Freedom*. Forrest delivers one of the eulogies at Ralph Ellison's funeral in April.

1995    W. W. Norton releases *Divine Days* in paperback.

1997    Forrest succumbs to cancer on November 6 at the age of 60.

2001    Northwestern University Press releases *Meteor in the Madhouse*, a collection of novellas Forrest completed before his death.

Conversations with Leon Forrest

# "If He Changed My Name": An Interview with Leon Forrest

Maria K. Mootry / 1975

From *Chant of Saints: A Gathering of Afro-American Literature, Art, and Scholarship* (1979). © 1979 by Michael S. Harper and Robert B. Stepto. Reprinted by permission.

**Maria K. Mootry:** Your novel *There Is a Tree More Ancient Than Eden* is a highly experimental work. I see in it a montage of narrative styles: the reflexive language of poetry, the immediacy of dramatic monologue and the high rhetoric and eloquence of the Afro-American sermon tradition. Do you think style in itself is a message?

**Leon Forrest:** If a writer attempts to approach his materials in an imaginative manner, more than likely he's going to be inventive about the mode he casts them in . . . the manner in which he reshapes or structures those "story-laden," symbolic patterns of human essence, culled from the consciousness of the family, race, and nation. Certainly this is true with much of the great literature, and the author-models of technical power, whose works I found fascinating long before I attempted to write, and probably upon whose shoulders I have climbed, in order to attempt an entry into the ring of champions. All were master stylists to be sure: Joyce, Proust, Twain. Hawthorne, Melville, Faulkner, Dylan Thomas, and Mr. Ralph Ellison. These craftsmen were my principal literary mentors, and in the main, I am proud to say, authors who raised the moral questions and the spectre of moral hypocrisy.

**M:** Now you sound like Ellison protesting that the "greats" were his masters. Aren't there black roots in your work?

**F:** Yes, for behind all of this was the nourishing information and *intelligence* of the spirituals, jazz, and the blues, and their influence and ground-swelling shaping of my consciousness and my sense of the possibilities of form, black life, responsibility and challenge, and of course style in grand Negro manner, and finally the Afro-American ranges of eloquence, in the pulpit and on the platter. As a child I used to listen to my parents' fine record collection. My mother loved the vocalists, and understood what was happening, for instance, in Holiday's art. Again, on my mother's side there is the New Orleans influence particularly about jazz, and my uncle George White, who was and still is a kind of walking legend about early jazz. My father was greatly interested in what the instrumentalists were doing. Also my father knew or had met many of the great musicians, like Cootie Williams, on the old Santa Fe Railroad, the Super Chief, where he served for many years as a bartender. And he brought that kind of information home, in terms of his own thinking and his selection of records. But also my dad used to sing in the choir of Pilgrim Baptist church, and he was interested in the spiritual singing. He possessed a fine singing voice, started writing lyrics in his late twenties, and even recorded some of his songs.

**M:** I see something of a concern for excellence here . . .
**F:** Yes, there was always this tradition of doing it right, whatever you were doing, a sense of perfection—which when you deal with it from the old time Negro perspective was not only obsessional, but linked to survival or death. . . . Added to all of this many-sided nourishment was an inordinate number of gifted story-tellers and liars on both sides of the family. . . . And always a sense of standards and style and substance, if you were scrubbing a floor, or lying, or generally attempting to stand tall and be counted in the world, and a sense that if your standards were up and elevated that of course you would be making a contribution. . . . Perhaps what I loved in Ray "Sugar" Robinson's athletic artistry was exactly this combination of excellence, style, and artistry. Now I doubt if Mr. Robinson has read my novel (or will ever read any of my novels; I would be honored if he did, of course), but I always want it to embrace the traditions I learned from him and others: this will to win, to be the best, no matter what you attempted. . . .

**M:** Most of *Tree* is set in Chicago. Nathaniel's birthdate would, I gather, be approximately your own, and the dominating theme of the loss of a parent coincides with your personal experience. There seems to be an autobiographical element in the novel, but I'm wondering if you found achieving a proper distance a problem?
**F:** Well, since it all leapt out of my head, I guess it's all autobiographical; and I'll claim that child . . . [laughs] . . . Seriously, though, knowing or not

knowing whether the writer (who is always a liar) considers the book highly autobiographical, or slightly so, doesn't help the critic one damn bit in solving the literary questions of the novel which is an imaginative act. Perhaps it is more important for the critic to know those well-springs of nourishment from whence the artist's materials derive than the biographical material. . . . And I'm not a new writer. I'd been writing about fifteen years before *Tree* was published. . . . *Wood-shedding,* you might say. The writer can't be concerned about distance, only how to win the championship, the title (in fifteen rounds or less)—fifteen chapters or less and how to marshal his killer instinct (a combination of the super-ego and the ego) which he or she must possess, or be doomed to the amateur ranks forever. What's more important than autobiography is the continuity of the writer's kind of mind, which is universal. . . . You are talking about a highly associative kind of memory-mind; a highly reflective person, who does his work in isolation, and trains his mind—his imagination—on books and folklore. He must have a love and a fury for work, work, and re-working. He must love re-writing the way an actor loves rehearsals. For finally literature is about the projection of a vision of life, and as he re-writes endlessly he comes to gain a control over the chaos of his materials which floods up from his unconscious.

**M:** I'm wondering whether your experiences as a journalist helped or hindered your work.
**F:** Well, as I suggested earlier, during much of the writing of *There Is a Tree,* I was working in editorial positions, sometimes at half the salary of a beginning journalist, with the daily papers—even though I had been in the field for ten years. Even in the last years my salary was only half that of a managing editor at a larger metropolitan newspaper. But the freedom to go for broke on the hard issues of the '60s and early '70s, in a field that is so corralling, was quite attractive to me. I lived the semi-dormitory life of the apprentice writer, in the early years of that news career, which the young writer must be willing to go through. I was unmarried, still rather young; yet not so young either. But I could absorb the surface protest of my firelight there at the newspapers, so that in the evenings I was forced to seek out the soul of black folk, at a deeper level for the soul-meat of my fictional vision. Then too, even in the early days editors usually got me writing features, figuring I was either too dumb or too imaginative to write straight news. But this worked in my favor, in terms of the fiction, because it took me back to my love of language—allowed me to play around with words in the

features—yet forced upon me a continual sense of the compactness of language and structure. . . . The organizational possibilities in a brief space; also, of course, quick character delineation. ("Give me a feature story, Forrest, in three pages or less on this guy.")

I was rarely in a position of putting out stuff in a soup-line or mill-factory situation. Thus, I never was confronted with the perils of becoming a hack, although if I had stayed around long enough, ultimately that might have happened. Still as you get older your energies wane, and I would hate to have come home from a day of writing to tackle a novel. . . . One of the hundreds of reasons why so much of the so-called black protest writing of the 1960s is a bore today, comes from the fact that much of it was not about coming consciousness at all, but rather emotional, narcissistic, one-dimensional heat, perhaps only simple letters-to-the-editor, in the form of limericks. Leaving aside the question of talent, some might have been saved, if they had been forced to empty out that surface outrage in some form, and then got down to that Body and Soul in their fiction, or poetry.

**M:** Have you experimented with other genres?
**F:** Well I started off wanting to write poetry, and I did for a time. I went through a longer period writing plays and thinking that I had found a home. I wanted to write verse-plays. But being a snob, I stupidly declined to work in the theatre. An absolute essential for the playwright.

**M:** Yes. And today more than ever black theatre is being projected as community theatre for a community audience. Do you write for any particular audience?
**F:** No. I only write for people who are interested in serious literature.

**M:** *Tree* is peopled by several striking personalities. There is, of course, the indomitable, yea-saying Auntie Breedlove; there are also several memorable lesser figures. What do you try to do in creating character?
**F:** Well I'm always trying to find their own true voice . . . not to dominate them or get in their way. They have a right to their own lives, and if that right is worthy to be presented before the reader, then it's my responsibility to get the hell out of their mouths and let them do the talking. I try not to push Forrest off on them, always to approach them with respect, and present them in their broadest possible dimensions.

**M:** Perhaps it was a personal predilection, but I noticed a bird/angel/flight pattern of imagery permeating the novel. I was reminded of other writers who incorporated similar dichotomies in their fictions. In Ellison's much-anthologized short story, "Flying Home," for instance, the rather naive aspiring black pilot is forced into an ignominious landing. Once on the ground he is forced to deal with his rural, ancestral past. Or, in the case of Nigerian writer, Wole Soyinka, the protagonist of his novel *The Interpreters*, while aspiring to climb a social ladder, nearly "drowns" in an ancestral grove. There seems to be a multiple dialectic going on in which social, spiritual and metaphysical longings are countered by the awareness of the character's lowly social origins, his demanding flesh, and his "human" epistemology. Do you feel that this kind of imagery has special meaning in black history and culture?

**F:** I am always trying to bring into my work those images or motifs that seem to have sustained themselves longest in the culture, black and white. Some of this is quite conscious and some of it isn't at all. But I think the danger, always for me at least, is that the language and imagery come rather rapidly, and sometimes are highly personal, ergo, a peril, for I learned long ago never to trust anything that comes easy. In order to test the image, I must set that part of the writing aside for a while and go back again, lest my writing become victimized by what I guess must be my long suit, if I have a long suit. But those that you mentioned are out of the black experience, I am always trying to see how many shapes and sides I can squeeze from the images; that's perhaps another long distance test of their life, and my skill or lack of skill.

**M:** You have cited Joyce and Faulkner, "mainstream" writers, as writers whose work you most admire. Do you feel that being in an African American department is somewhat problematical? Do you get an itch to teach a course, say on Hemingway or Joyce or Faulkner?

**F:** No. My basic itch about Hemingway, Joyce, or Faulkner is to beat them. Write better works. I'm only completing my second year at Northwestern so I might do a great many things before I leave. Might even teach journalism. But I do teach Faulkner in a class entitled: The Oral Tradition and the Creative Process . . . I use his *Sound and the Fury*. I also use his work in my novel class—*Light in August*. I am still shaping the oral tradition class; and next year I'll be using some of Achebe, the Nigerian novelist, when we discuss the Oral Tradition in terms of the West African writers. In another course, I shall teach Joyce and Hemingway and Faulkner incorporated along with Baldwin, Ellison, Toomer, and Forrest and Murray. This novel course will be about sensibility, initiation as manifested and revealed in language, as *the* motif shaper of coming wakefulness—regional, ethnic, and personal. Actually, I am the only member in the department who teaches under introductory studies *and* English department aegis, and when I was hired the dean asked me what I wanted to teach. . . . And of course I will continue to teach what I want to teach. Just as I write what I want to write. But, on the other hand, I would not teach certain novels of Faulkner's, just as there are novels by black writers that I would not teach now, because I don't feel enough about them or because I am not knowledgeable enough about them. I only itch to teach those writers whose work will fit into the thrust of my class and will be helpful to my students.

**M:** It seems that many writers today are affiliated with some university. Do you see a positive relation between teaching and writing, or does your role as an academician conflict with your role as an artist?
**F:** I am not an academic. I talk literary techniques in classes as I have learned, and incorporated them in my own writings . . . I am an artist and for that kind of writer, life is never compartmentalized. The teaching techniques—literary craft knowledge in my case—that I employ in the classroom are related to those techniques I employ on paper, at home before the typewriter. The university is, can be, a nourishing center for thought. This is the place where the Word is taught and standardized and sanctified in the libraries and in the classroom; I try to reshape, purify, standardize, and sanctify language in my own way. And you have been most generous in your responses to my failed attempts in this regard. But you see, Maria, one of my visions as a black artist is the sense of ancestral responsibility, of purifying the language to get our eloquence and rounded felt-life in the center of the arena. Now the more serious modern writers, the men who have gone before me, like Ellison and Bellow, are back in the university for the possible intellectual nourishment and development so necessary for the writer in the second and third stages of his development. The university supplies the place for us that newspapers once furnished for writers, in terms of intellectual content, writing excellence, the tension between the fierce street-life contests, and how to re-order all of that at the typewriter. Many of these newsmen were really

fiction writers, who had no other way to support themselves, and the news-paper-reading public benefited greatly from the material under their by-lines. The university doesn't have to be the entrapping monolith it was perhaps at one time. One can still get back out on the streets. It's entirely up to you.

**M:** You teach two of N. Scott Momaday's novels in your course on American Indian writing. Are the problems of Native American writing and writers similar to those of the black writing and writers? Is there a debate among American Indian *literati* similar to that among blacks?
**F:** Momaday is on the list for the same reasons Faulkner and Ellison are there: all three have broken out of the narrows of land, regionalism, or racial entrapment and have given us the broadest kind of vision of life. My students (I have never unfortunately had any Native Americans in my classes) enjoy Momaday because, while he celebrates the *Indianness* of his people, honoring their strengths and castigating their weaknesses, he offers a vision of modern man's terror-riddled complexities in the virtual no-man's land that is America. . . . Momaday is on the list because he celebrates much of the rich-ness of Indian folklore. And of course there is some universality about all folklore at its richest. . . . Recently I have been doing some things in both my class work and my new novel with the Orpheus myth. There is a complete watershed cycle of materials on that Indian-variation of the Orpheus myth, which stretches from one end of the country to the other.

**M:** How do Native Americans respond to this universal-in-particular?
**F:** Now, Momaday is not so popular among certain Indians, just as Ralph Ellison is unpopular with some blacks. Because they think that the soul of the Race, the over-riding power, the anguish and the protest is lodged away in the narrows, in the provincial aspects of the group. I understand this. But, my job as an artist, and I imagine Mr. Momaday must feel this way, is to get the major projected vision into that literary arena, and compete with my peers working the modern novel, today. Momaday's Indian critics don't like the fact he has received all of this applause by whites. So Momaday is not univer-sally loved. But many Jews don't like Bellow either, because they feel Bellow gives up too much of the ethnic thing as he reaches out to touch the condi-tion of modern man (with the use of the wandering Jewish intellectual, with all of the old pratfalls of the Jewish monologue-spiel character, speeding along from one fool's errand to next) in the hellish wilderness of North

America. They like Malamud much better. He's closer to their Jewishness. Yet in a name-dropping contest they would probably mention meeting Saul Bellow much more than Malamud.

**M:** Are there pressures on Native American writers to be more political?
**F:** I met a leading Native American intellectual at a conference recently who was quite critical of Momaday for going to Moscow University to teach for a period of time and not staying here for the war his people must fight for liberation. . . . Now where have you heard that before?

**M:** Yes, sounds familiar. Where are we in the development of Native American fiction.
**F:** There just have not been that many first-rate novels by Indian Americans. First-rate in the way Momaday is first-rate. But a monumental body of folklore is there for the writer to develop and build from. Much of the most interesting writing too, like ours, has been autobiography, or biography, rather than fiction. But like the blacks, when the revolutionary talk of the '60s went down, volumes of misinformation tumbled down upon the scenes. Well, themes such as identity crisis, alienation and affirmation from the past and by the past, the role of the ancestral intelligence, the conflict over the quest for a personality center that's meaningful, the role of liberals in the struggle; these are some of the questions that are quite similar to the questions faced by black writers—in some ways all American writers. . . . But black writers have the especial duty to reveal how our people have been dominant carriers and reshapers in a very fundamental way in the cultural life of America. . . . Then too, the blacks have a thriving and active middle and upper-middle class, from which much of our institutional leadership derives, and which is highly American and highly proud of its combined heritage. Indians don't have this.

**M:** Getting back to your position as a member of an African American department, how would you assess the impact of black studies on black and white students? And what would you predict for black studies?
**F:** Well in order to survive, departments will have to deal with the universities on a highly sophisticated level, demand that their staffs be culled from the best people available, and not the rhetorical bullshit artists. They'll have to get more and more involved in the general life of the campus—dominate it

intellectually and in terms of inventive vitality. They'll have to make up their minds to intellectually dominate reality, the American reality. The administrations *knew* if they laid in the cut and waited, student apathy would save them from having to deal with the formidable question of the absence of black heritage in the intellectual life of the university. So that the departments can't depend on the students to fight battles with the university—not in today's atmosphere. Black students by and large simply aren't competitive enough. And when we suggest the literature of blacks is complicated, complicated in the way we are as a people, many don't want to hear. The white students are more competitive on the average and do better.

**M:** There is a continuing debate on the allegiances or non-allegiances of the artist. Do you think a writer should use his art to change society?
**F:** That presumes of course that he knows anything about anything other than writing sentences, creating lasting metaphors, and memorable characters. But we Americans assume because a man is good at one thing he is the man to answer the call of a discipline of highly developed techniques and skills, even if he is without training. Most writers work alone—even to some extent if you write musicals. Politics and social or societal changes must connect with day-in-and-day-out power, persuasion, struggle, and cunning, and have the capacity to deliver a rather constant set of immediate victories for a group of people. . . . Some writers perhaps can do all of that but most can't, even when they say they can. . . . Most times they don't have the craft, knowledge, the staying power, the constituency, the temperament, the mind-set.

**M:** In other words there is a fundamental difference between the artist and the activist?
**F:** Well, all we know for certain is that said writer has an interesting way of re-telling the old stories with new renditions. He's an imaginative editor with a projected vision of life that is so stunning we can't ever put down the book, at best . . . that he has reassembled a body of techniques over the chaos of materials abounding, and given us a new, haunting order and vision of our days upon this planet, even as he links our outrage, sense of tragedy and delight to the battle of our common ancestral search for Home, Freedom, Power, and Love. Well now, if he can do simply that, that a glory it would be.

**M:** In short, you would agree with the aestheticians that the artist's province is that of the mind and the imagination. . . .

**F:** That's the point. Now that same man might be a damn fool doing anything else, and don't you just know the political masters are going to laugh him off the floor of Congress. Also the question presumes of course that the writer can wield power in the immediate marketplace, jobs, crash welfare programs, political might, diplomatic grace, and that he knows something about technical grace and statecraft in a meaningful way, rather than a sophomoric way.

**M:** Then, where would a cultural essayist like James Baldwin enter into the picture? Is his type of intellectual barrage the best example of art as protest?

**F:** Now about Jimmy Baldwin . . . those essays of the fifties and early sixties worked so neatly in concert with the whole fashioning of a people's instrument towards political freedom, accommodations, voting rights, etc. And they were very significant in terms of re-enlightening rather enlightened, articulate white (and some black) readers in powerful, fairly stimulating journals, left of center (like *Esquire* or *Harper's*), as the Movement itself called upon the conscience of the best in the freedom traditions of the country. Those essays worked well in terms of the total Freedom Movement gearshift, which came down hard, yet smoothly with grace (like Jimmy's essays), on the guilt of America—but those propaganda essays worked best upon the highly influential, radical chic of that day, people who had powerful political links. . . . They were one dimension of a many-sided sword. But, when Bull Connor let those dogs loose on black people, that touched the heart albeit ever so fleetingly, of white people who had never read Baldwin. . . . Those essays were brilliant, immediate, but read today (after we got the rights, but not always the implementation) those essays, in the main, only stand up as good examples of the inventive construct of essay writing, in which Baldwin incorporated many of the techniques of the novelist. . . . Jimmy didn't know any deep history or have any deep political thought or any economic theories. . . . So, most of those essays now seem more like period pieces of the historical town-crier, addressed as Baldwin might say to a "grievously hypocritical Republic."

**M:** Well, most people think Baldwin's essays are superior to his fiction. Do you agree?

**F:** Not quite. Now, what was addressed to our long-haul story was a fine book, called *Go Tell It on the Mountain*. That book was never a part of the

Civil Rights Freedom Movement's war-chest of immediacy, and frontal assaults, as were his essays. Yet *Go Tell It* apparently endures; it is literature. And it has within its resources the eloquence of literature, the imperishable hallmarks that a people might hold onto, and be uplifted by, and challenged through. That's a possible function of literature. A people can endure through it. *And*, with all of this talk about black survival nobody talks much about the possibilities of institutional inner strength in terms of what a great book can continually give a people, as they (generation after generation) read and re-read into its depths, and *their* depths. A book like *Invisible Man* keeps enriching the individual and informing him or her with each new reading about the human condition, the human predicament. . . .

**M:** Have any writers influenced you more than others?
**F:** I might think that one writer influenced me to an extent far greater than was actually the case. . . . Recently I've become quite interested in the minor influences of Hemingway upon Faulkner's work, particularly in certain sardonic understated dialogue scenes, for instance Max and Mame (and Bobbie) in *Light in August*—some of that dialogue. . . . Well, most people don't ever think of those writers together since they are so different; yet the influence is there. But, don't forget Hemingway was an all but universally acknowledged master of the short-story some time before Faulkner was to completely find himself, or shape his art.

But what's more important is the body of work, over the long haul, and the folklore which informs the intelligence of the people who nourish the author's art.

**M:** The multiplicity of black consciousnesses. . . .
**F:** Yes, you see the writer is a vulture in the sense that he'll feed on almost anything that can give him and his art nourishment—hopefully he'll have better taste than the vulture. I've said that he is a liar, and let me add that he is also a thief. . . . On the other hand, the whole nourishment from culture and form, from all the shapes he gets from other writers, from the weather, architecture, music, sculpture, is so implicit that only a critic, looking over an extended body of a writer's work, can point out, scientifically, the levels of influences. There you can take into account the body of literature which nourished a writer's earliest development; that's more important, since any first-rate writer reads a range of work that may basically touch his sense of form, or shape his language, but not affect his heart-core storehouse of

character associations and the soul and guts of his own art. . . . For instance I couldn't see how Henry James has influenced me; but he strongly shaped Baldwin's essay/novel prose.

**M:** Today there is a wider range of black writing than ever before. Do you consider yourself part of a "school" in black writing?
**F:** Well, McPherson, Morrison, Murray, Ellison, Wideman, and I are all club-members you might say.

**M:** What advice would you give to an aspiring black writer?
**F:** Well, clearly he must develop a writer's mind, which is highly associative—and deeply reflective—and constantly see story material possibilities in patterns, in symbolic connections, word transitions in the world about him, and within him. He must develop a fury for re-writing, for it is only via re-writing, endlessly, obsessively, that he can ever write into currents of energy, felt-knowledge memories. The writer's mind is possessed by a long and deep memory of the way things fit or are in paradox, but he must train his mind to find his form. He must be extremely ambitious—must possess a "Killer-instinct," I believe—in that he is constantly thinking: well now, Joyce did it this way; or Faulkner did it this way. . . . Always testing himself against the masters, always thinking in terms of that—of the giants. How good I must be if I am going up against this champion. He must read constantly and nourish himself upon varied sources of reading. You're talking about an extremely stubborn intelligence—but because writing is the loneliest of the arts, the highest and the most demanding, and in our country the most spat-upon, and seriously regarded as a n oddity, he had better be very stubborn. His writing must be nourished upon a storehouse of materials, which come form what he has read, what he has observed, and what he has experienced. But the life of the imagination is the most important, central complexity that he must develop.

**M:** Thank you very much.

# Leon Forrest at the University of Kentucky: On *The Bloodworth Orphans*

John G. Cawelti / 1988

**Cawelti:** It's a great pleasure to introduce Leon Forrest. I've asked him to start out with a few remarks on how he came to write *The Bloodworth Orphans*.

**Forrest:** I thank Dr. Cawelti for inviting me. It may be helpful to know I had published a novel called *There Is a Tree More Ancient than Eden* the year before in 1973. I wanted to write a book that was filled with character and characterization. My first novel was very impressionistic. It tried to capture the consciousness of African American people in this country, or some of it anyway, in an impressionistic novel influenced by *Portrait of the Artist* and other works. Almost as an answer to the critics of *There Is a Tree*, I wanted to create a novel filled with characters and a lot of character development. That was one impetus to *The Bloodworth Orphans*. The other was the idea of doing something on families. I was influenced not only by Faulkner, but by O'Neill and the rising sense of the crisis in the Afro-American family—indeed the American family. It was another genesis issue. Another was that in my family, there are any number of patterns of orphans: people who have taken in orphans, either by adopting them or raising them or otherwise helping them. This was particularly true of the Catholic side of my family (through the Catholic Family Bureau in Chicago). This gets enriched by the other side of my family tree, which is Protestant and Baptist on my father's side. In the Afro-American extended family any number of people that we knew were brought into the family preserves and raised, even though they were not related to us. They call the older people "aunt, uncle, etc."—of course, that also has a southern genesis. Calling people aunt and uncle and cousin gets back to the connection of Negroes and whites in the south. So there is always this kind of Southern black-like connection in groups.

There is an additional source. I was brought into the university community at that time, and moved from being a newspaper man to being associate professor of African American studies at Northwestern. I came into the university mainly with the idea of broadening my intellectual perspective. The writers I admired most, Ellison, Baldwin, and Malamud had returned to the university and none were academics in the traditional sense. They had desperately sought in this American society so bereft of intellectual life to find some place of intellectual vibrancy.

At one time in this country, creative writers wrote for newspapers. Many of them are now working with universities. This really started after World War II. When the opportunity developed to come to Northwestern and teach, I thought this would be a possibility of growth. One of the interesting things about writers in this country, in this century (perhaps separating us from Henry James), is the fact that many of our writers didn't finish college. I didn't finish college, either. I thought that one thing which separated us from the European and Russian novelists was that somehow our education was incomplete. I thought by going back to the university, I might complete that side of my education. What I didn't understand was that the writer lives a life of trying to complete his or her education. It is never completed. That is what I try to convey to my students at Northwestern in undergraduate school as well as in continuing education. At any rate, this experience got me to reading in a serious and a critical way works that I had read in a more general way. I was reading at the time several sources that go into this book. I was first assigned that task of trying to connect Afro-American literature and Native American writing. I got very interested in reading and rereading certain Native American writers. That got me back to the mythical aspects of traditional cultures. I became quite fascinated by the Orpheus myth, which appears in many many ways, in black culture, the movie *Black Orpheus* for instance. The myth is about this extraordinary musician in love with this extraordinary woman and she dies and goes to the land of the underground and the only way he can repatriate her is to sing her out a hymn. This spoke to me about Nat King Cole, Billy Eckstine and all these fantastic black singers. How many of your parents or grandparents fell in love while listening to some extraordinary black singer. I come from a people of singers and I have always been attracted to the great singers in literature. The great Irish writers are so helpful here. Joyce and O'Casey and O'Faolain, the great short story writer, that I read in high school. Of course the brilliance of Yeats. This led me to another great influence in my work and that is Dylan Thomas, who is connected as a Welshman to both the Irish heritage and the English. All of that became more vivid in my imagination now that I was at the university where I could read these people critically and intellectually and try to teach them. I was teaching things about oral tradition, not only out of my own heritage but also of the heritage that I also share as a westerner and also the Old Testament. This went into the formation of *The Bloodworth Orphans.*

Another element was the influence of Ellison and Faulkner. *The Invisible Man* and *The Sound and the Fury* are kind of similar works in my own development. In Ellison, it was important for me to see, for perhaps the first time, a black writer who took on the problems of how you translate the oral tradition into the eloquence of traditional literature. Ellison was the black novelist who was able to do this. Faulkner, who also comes out of a highly oral tradition, had the same problems and he was instructive in this. For instance, Faulkner has this extraordinary sermon that you have read in *The Sound and the Fury* of Rev. Shegog. I knew a lot about sermons through both of my heritages . . . my three heritages . . . my Afro-American-Protestant heritage, my Catholic heritage and of course the writers who had developed sermons in their works, such as Melville, and *Moby Dick* and then of course, Faulkner and Rev. Shegog's sermon. To me, it was just the starting of what I wanted to do. I wanted to do the broadest kind of thing in sermons. Ellison and Faulkner opened up for me the possibility of not only of how you can make a sermon novelistic and how that sermon can be the key to the novel.

Perhaps the third thing would be the connection with James Weldon Johnson, the black writer, who collected a group of sermons. That was oral tradition. I felt that I wanted to move past oral tradition to written tradition. Another key that Ellison offered me was the connection to Lord Raglan and his extraordinary book *The Hero* which was written by a man who was not a trained anthropologist, but who took on that idea of exploring other cultures. Oftentimes, clues to what you are doing can come from someone completely outside of your culture. Your culture, if you are deeply involved in it and if you are American, presents you with a sense of chaos. We are a nation of chaos. If you are an artist, you must make something of chaos, and turn it into art. It is absolutely essential; you will die as an artist or as a man or a woman if you can't do that. You will die, you will kill yourself, if you can't do that privately. All the great artists who killed themselves did so because ultimately they couldn't do it. Your drive is to make some order of this chaos, and oftentimes the clue to this comes from cultures outside of yours. That's one of the ironies of it. Lord Raglan presents a concept of the hero that has become very important to me, along with Ellison's notions about the hero. I was also reading (Heinrich) Zimmers's *King and the Corpse*, and much Eastern literature with the idea of gaining some sense of leverage over the chaos of Afro-American life. I haven't satisfied that and probably won't satisfy that.

In general, I wanted to use the sermon as a means of looking into the whole agony of being Afro-American. I wanted to suggest the spiritual, political, social, and intellectual dynamics of what it meant to be an American. Perhaps I've failed at that, but why is the country so caught up with the preacher? Where did he come from? Throughout my work I've been fascinated with the eloquence of the preacher and with the idea of working my way from oral eloquence to written eloquence, linking that to the problems of identity, of religion, of politics, and culture in society and making it a springboard within my own culture. Those were some of the issues I was involved with.

I wrote many scenes in the novel as monologues. I was very much interested in monologues. Here again Ellison, Faulkner, and Dostoyevsky were very helpful. Also the tradition of monologue in our society, the preacher or the comedian—the standup comedian, who expresses his soul through monologue. This is probably the reason there are so many monologues in the world. The idea is that you can express a whole range of life, an epic, a world in a monologue. That was part of what intrigued me about monologues. I started *The Bloodworth Orphans* with the monologue of Carl-Rae Bowman. It happens early in the novel. He is a loose man and as I remember (it has been a long time), one of the two sons of Rachel Flowers, the two sons she had by a white man in the south. The other one was Industrious. You hear Carl-Rae's last dying monologue there in a garbage can. There is this woman who is trying to save him then but he is a wanderer and a drifter and a lost man. Of course, that is the case with many of the lost souls in this novel and I was very inspired at that time, since it was the first thing I wrote in the novel.

After I left the Muslim paper *Muhammad Speaks*, I worked at home before I went out to Northwestern. I used to go home at night and listen to this song by the extraordinary blues singer Lyman Hoffman. There are some wonderful lines in it and some of them are "On this next train south, you can look for my clothes home but if you don't see my body, Mama, all you can do is mourn." That just haunted me all over. Every night I would go home and rewrite it. My method of writing is to take the most basic kind of line and improvize on it. After all, I am the child of the culture which created jazz. I would just take that line and improvize on it again and again and develop this monologue from it. "On that next train south, you can look for my clothes home. But if you don't see my body, Mama, all you can do is mourn." That got me into the idea of Carl-Rae and the relationship to his mother, and then out of that I began to develop many of the other themes of orphans. I had finished a stay with the Black Muslims and one of their themes was always the idea that Afro-Americans were a lost-found nation. I didn't agree with most of what the movement said but one thing they stood for was the idea that Afro-Americans were a lost-found people in this country. It seems to me that that was a very ironic statement since no one in this society is more American than blacks.

I worked on that theme of orphans with Carl-Rae and that brought in the orphans in my own family and the idea that blacks came to this country and were sold and shipped around and constantly given a sense of being orphans. Ultimately, after the Civil War, the greatest quest among black Americans was to find their homes and find who they belonged to. The song which Regal Pettibone loves to sing should perhaps be the theme song of black America. "Sometimes I feel like a motherless child."

I would be glad to answer any questions.

**Student:** Is this large number of orphans a result of breakdowns within the black family, or is it a broader thing of blacks being brought to this country and being abandoned by the white society?
**Forrest:** Blacks were forcibly brought into this country and separated early on from their families and their fathers. The search for wholeness and harmony in family emanates from that. But that is not only our condition as black Americans but if afflicts all Americans as this society is played out. In an immediate sense, we can say the black American family is in trouble, which it is for sure. But also the American family is in trouble, and the quest for the father is a very vital contemporary concern. When I thought about contemporary life and contemporary black American life the idea of orphans

seemed everywhere. I wanted to engage not only the Afro-American past, but contemporary issues. I was also hoping and dreaming, as any writer worth his (her) salt does, that my work would be something that would be helpful or useful to my country.

**Student:** You mentioned an interest in O'Neill. I'm interested in the monologue. Do you see yourself primarily as a dramatist or as working that into the modern novel. Do you have any interest in doing something on the stage or will you continue to write novels?

**Forrest:** Initially, I wanted to be a poet. I wrote poetry for a long time, but I didn't have the discipline. That was part of the influence of Yeats, but particularly of Dylan Thomas and his use of monologues and how you could move from all eloquence in general (Dylan Thomas's father was a preacher) to a kind of literary style. I wanted to be a playwright for a long time. I wrote plays and I had one or two produced in reader-style theater. My problem was that I wouldn't work in the theater. I was a snob. Of course you have to work in theater to learn the problems of theatre. Our greatest playwrights have taught us this. Our greatest playwrights Shakespeare, Ibsen, Tennessee Williams, etc. I finally found out that what I was really in love with, after all, was the beauty of dramatic language. I wanted to try to keep alive all these interests, anyway, both in poetry and monologue and theater. I finally came to writing novels. A friend of mine, sort of a running buddy of mine, was in theatre, used to read my work, and he read an extraordinarily long play of mine once and he said "Leon, this is a novel, this isn't a play." It was the love of dramatic literature that I have tried to keep alive in my work. Probably more than I realized I was influenced by Strindberg, which I remembered loving so much. Strindberg was so helpful in these monologues. And Tennessee Williams with these extraordinary monologues of those great ladies. Well, I love ladies too. I also loved them in novels. O'Neill was helpful too, because O'Neill, like Faulkner was always dealing with relationships and emotions of family which lie beneath the surface, which are part of a kind of secret heritage that one does not want to admit. The playwrights were very important and I was also interested in the early '60s before I finally made my last transition in the British playwrights in that wonderful group of Osborne and the angry writers of the British theater and again you think about some extraordinary monologues there. So this was all a part of it.

**Student:** Have you a collection of your plays? Are they published?
**Forrest:** No, they are not, but one long play was presented in reader-style theater and I did incorporate some of it in my first novel *There Is a Tree More Ancient than Eden*. The monologue that was by Madge Ann Fishbond. She also showed up in *The Bloodworth Orphans*. I was working as a journalist through all of this. I had this kind of background to work on when I turned to my fiction. Though the protests of the '60s were influential, I thought that the monologue would help me to get into the interior of characters. So often, no one got into the complexity of the black character. I don't think we have touched the surface of his complexity.

The other thing that I tried to do was to move past some of the people who had influenced me. O'Neill connected me with the Irish tradition and Irish literature, which I had already been interested in through reading Yeats and Sean O'Casey. Like African Americans the Irish had the experience of living as a suppressed people, and having to take over the language of the conqueror. This is the way black Americans have taken basketball from white people. They have taken the damn thing over. That's what I wanted to do with writing. Take it over. I learned something about that from the Irish.

**Student:** I was very impressed by the sentence structure of your prose. I have noticed that it is more or less similar to Faulkner. Did you find yourself consciously using Faulkner's style as a model?
**Forrest:** I would be a liar and a fool to deny the influence of all I have read. Faulkner was certainly a strong influence, in general. Hardy was a great influence in high school (at Hyde Park); later on South American writers, especially Gárcia Márquez influenced me. But I think Faulkner also showed me a way of breaking open the sentence structure and opening it up so you could go for broke in it. That also helped with the monologues. Of course I was very interested in Faulkner's idea of a mythical kingdom, which also goes back to Hardy. Also, Faulkner's sensitivity to black life in a general way and his understanding of some aspects of the complexity of these relationships. I am certainly not the person to say how far I have gone past Faulkner in creating my own. Faulkner could certainly say, as Charlie Parker once said, that all musicians coming after him would have to pay their dues to him. I certainly have to pay my dues to Faulkner and I don't know if I have gone beyond him or not.

He certainly is an extraordinary influence and I am not the only writer influenced by Faulkner. Styron was, much more than I am; Toni Morrison, very much so; Ellison, Albert Murray. I think the best of Faulkner is involved with black life. With the exception of *As I Lay Dying*, it's only when he deals with this negro presence, that he is onto the tragedy of the south, and indeed this country. Faulkner also is very helpful in terms of clues. You can mention what he did with Rev. Shegog's sermon, for example. I have to go beyond that. There's certainly this competition as Faulkner himself said, "The young writer if he is worth his salt, he wants to beat the old guy." But it's hard to be a better hitter than Ted Williams.

**Student:** Could you tell us what you see as the central theme of *The Bloodworth Orphans*?

**Forrest:** I would say that the novel is about African Americans trying to find a home and the difficulty of that, the difficulty of ever finding some home. In the search for that and the chaos of it. Maybe Africa and the South came together to make this new people—Afro-Americans—in this country. My own thought is that this is ultimately being an American. For Americans, there are none of these ultimate touchstones that you can say are home. You carry home with you. This is what Thomas Wolfe perhaps didn't understand. You carry home with you and you keep going into new territory and facing new problems and chaos and you don't know how much of the old world will keep you alive.

**Student:** Gospel music seems to play an important part in your work. Could you discuss that?

**Forrest:** There is a powerful relationship between sexuality and spirituality which seems to me to be the glory and the power of negro gospel music. This marriage of sexuality and spirituality is at the heart of gospel music which is a union between the blues and the spiritual. At one time the notion was in black life that you could never mingle the two. Blues singers would say "Well, you just keep these separate." For a long time, in the middle-class Baptist churches in the north, people like Mahalia Jackson were not allowed. Ultimately, gospel music became important because there was a need to somehow bring together the secular and the spiritual, to find a kind of art form to match up with the growing complexity of black American life in the North.

**Student:** Your novel is so much concerned with chaos and disruption in the family. Do you see this as a special problem of African American life, or is this family violence more universal as a theme?

**Forrest:** I hope you will forgive me, for kind of a short handed answer to this excellent question. I was thinking about this after a book party for my last novel in April 1984. We had had a wonderful day and left this bookstore. Someone stopped us at the door, and said "you know, we just got word that Marvin Gaye was killed by his father." What a terrible family tragedy this was, almost like something Greek. We have a mother, father, and son in this house, which was built by the son. But the son is despised by the father, while the mother plays the two off against each other. Women and narcotics are also involved. But this is not just African American, it's contemporary America. It made me think, once again, that, in the most marvelous ways and in the most horrible ways black Americans are at the center of this society. I don't say this in any bragging. This may be why black American women writers are becoming more and more popular. Perhaps there's a sense that the experience they write about is deeply symbolic of our national experience. Just as when I was growing up Eugene O'Neill seemed so important. He was doing something similar for Irish families. So this whole theme of family chaos and disruption seemed to me suggestive of a broad range of American life.

**Cawelti:** In your third novel, *Two Wings to Veil My Face*, you deal with the experience of slavery, like Toni Morrison in her latest novel, *Beloved*, which has made such a tremendous impact on the American public, both white and black. Do you see this as a significant move in Afro-American literature, trying to imaginatively recapture that terrible era which has, until now, been largely absent from African American fiction. Unless I'm greatly mistaken, there was a period of slave narratives, Frederick Douglass, but that since then that time has been significantly avoided.

**Forrest:** That's true and I think there will be more of that. I think for me and maybe some of the others, it is a way for us, as Americans to see how entangled we are as a people with our heritage. In the novel *Two Wings to Veil My Face* the main character is a woman, who is 91. The novel is set in 1958. The woman was born two years after the end of the Civil War and four years after the Emancipation Proclamation. My own great-grandmother was born in 1877. I am 51 now. I knew many people, when I was coming along whose grandparents were slaves. It would be true of many people today. So, we are not that far removed from slavery. For the novelist with his larger sense of time, events that were a hundred years ago are not that long removed. Of course, we are still just coming out of the last shadows of the Civil War.

Many recent events suggest this. Jesse Jackson's campaign is a phenomenon which poses the question of whether we can elect to the presidency a man whose great-grandfather had been a slave. Generally, there's been very little from our great American writers on slavery. Obviously we have a rich harvest of histories but these are mainly by white historians. There were few black historians writing on slavery. But now, we are getting a sense of the complexity of the relationship between slaves and masters so I am interested in trying to evoke that and use that as a way of our understanding our own time. A hundred and twenty years is certainly not a long time in the life of a people, a race, or a country. Toni Morrison's last novel is very interested in that. I have been, continually. For me, the theme is more important as it is linked to families. There are many slave families, in this novel, and some of the characters in this novel who are also presented in my earlier works will probably continue to develop in my novels to come.

I think I am different from Haley in that I am interested in the human complexity of slavery and in what I can do with this as an artist. I like to let the imagination go wherever it might.

**Student:** What kind of similarities do you see in the black experience as captured by white writers and as captured by black ones, say Faulkner versus Ellison?

**Forrest:** Well, I don't know if I am a student of these things. In a general way, there is a general failure for me. Maybe I wouldn't be a writer if I didn't think earlier writers had failed, and I wanted to do something different. Most black writing and white writing about black characters is limited. And particularly when it involves black characters pitted against or in confrontation with whites. Of course, there have been certain extraordinary exceptions but some of the exceptional writers did this well on some occasions and didn't on others. I think Faulkner's successful in some things and he falls into very stereotypic characters in others. Richard Wright is oftentimes a failure. On occasion his characters are interesting and somewhat complex, but often they are less complex as characters and more important symbolically. Ellison's characters, in his one great novel, are always very intriguing. Certainly, William Styron's attempt to deal with Nat Turner was extraordinary. So, I want to look at the work. I don't care if its white or black. I don't agree that "If you're white, you can't write." I want to see what they can do. I also don't believe that because I am a man, I can't write about women. I had better quit writing, if I can't write about women. Why can't women write about men? It's talent that's important. Many southern whites could write rings around black northerners. It is true that some white writers have had a unique advantage. Faulkner had an extraordinary advantage that no black American has had that I can think of. He was able to walk around and touch every level of society. Poor white, black, white aristocracy, etc. though he didn't ever touch the black middle and upper middle class and that was his limitation. That's why you never see that in his writing. You would almost have to go back to Russian literature to find someone who could have the feel of every strata of the society. It is hard to imagine anyone having this today, because we are so separated and segregated in this society. Yet, Faulkner with his extraordinary talent did touch so many areas of Southern society and that allowed him to know all kinds of things about a wonderful range of black voices and black heritage. He had a sense of their rage for freedom. Where Faulkner stops is where a black writer should begin. Perhaps Joe Christmas is a good example of that. Often the black characters in Faulkner are symbolic more than they are fully developed characters, but his achievement is extraordinary. Many times the characters of Richard Wright are very limited, but, on occasion, he is really on to the great quest for freedom. Being good as a writer is a matter of how much you love the genre that you are working in and how much talent and drive and appetite for human character you have and your imagination and your willingness to take on things that you are attracted to and don't know all that much about. That's typical of novels. You want to write about something you know a little about but are attracted to, partly because it's so different from you.

**Student:** Does this mean that the writer must move beyond his personal experience?

**Forrest:** That's right. You burn out early on about autobiographical stuff. Your talent has to do with how much you can imagine in a felt way, in a yeasty way, in an emotional way. How much you can make your readers dream of reality, how much you can take over your readers' imagination. When you think about it, there's not an awful lot in what Rev. Shegog says in that sermon, but it's a powerful presence. That's Faulkner's talent.

**Student:** What do you think has influenced you most about your own background?

**Forrest:** I was raised Catholic on my mother's side and attended mass regularly. I didn't go to Catholic school, but I went to Catholic catechism classes one day a week on Wednesday. That's how I got my Catholic training in a specific way, so I could take first communion and get my confirmation. That's quite different from other cousins in my family. I used to spend regular weekends with the Protestant side of my family, my fathers' people, and go to church occasionally. Again, it has to do with the complexity of Afro-American culture. You might be divided between these worlds. From the Catholic side, I was always attracted to the ritual of it and to the grandness of the tradition, the concept of original sin and the secret self of confession. Maybe that's where my interior monologues come from. On the Protestant side, my father sang in the Pilgrim Baptist Church in the choir there and was leader of the junior choir. I became very interested, although I was not conscious of the interest as a child, in the thrust of negro spirituals and gospel music and the great sermons. As a matter of fact, the man of eloquence, someone like Jesse Jackson, and before him King, has a long heritage. One of the preachers in Chicago who was so eloquent and known nationally, though he wasn't connected with any kind of political movement was Rev. Austin (J. C. Austin) at he Pilgrim Baptist Church. President Roosevelt said he had the greatest speaking voice of any public man in America. His son is now the pastor of that church. Adam Clayton Powell was known for his power of eloquence. It was the Baptists on the Protestant side, that made me aware of eloquence as a form, not only a protest, but as it evoked the anguish and the celebration of black life on a larger stage. It wasn't writers, because after all, when I was coming along, there weren't that many well-known African American writers—*Invisible Man* wasn't published until the 50s and so on. It was the eloquence of these great public speakers, mainly preachers, and also the eloquence and style of black athletes that shaped me. It made me want to try to do something in a grand manner, in the grand style. It's apparent this caught some light in my imagination, when I started to write. Also, I was interested, from my Catholic side, in the New Testament. I used to read the epistles and the gospels to an invalid aunt of mine who couldn't go to mass on Sundays. My great grandmother, on my father's side, lived with us until I was about nine or ten and I used to read to her the Old Testament. I've gained much from these two heritages. For a long time I could never think about how I was going to write, because this all seemed to me to be rather chaotic. Anyway this was part of me. The Catholic side gets me back to New Orleans, my mother's people; my father's people, and the Protestant side, were from Mississippi. There is a long tradition, in Chicago, of blacks coming from Mississippi and Louisiana. What I tried to do was create an artistic version of that great migration.

**Student:** I have noticed that the current black women writers like Alice Walker have all acknowledged Zora Neale Hurston. You haven't mentioned her. Did she have any effect on you?

**Forrest:** No, because I didn't read her until I was in college. Of course, I've taught her regularly. I think your point is very important. There is a link between women writers like Hurston and Walker. You could go on with others like Toni Morrison. Hurston is sort of the grand mama for women writers, the way many white female writers would trace their lineage to Virginia Woolf. No, my linkage would be to Ellison and Faulkner. Of course, when I was in college, I began to know Hurston. Obviously, if you were talking to a black female writer, her perceptions would be different.

**Cawelti:** Well, we've got time for one more question. I would like you to talk about names. Names, seem to me one of the central themes in your work. Not only are you marvelously inventive in thinking up different names, but the recurrent phrase "he changed my name" seems to crop up very often in your novels.

**Forrest:** That is from a spiritual. "I asked Oh Jesus, if that was all right if He changed my name. And Jesus said, I would have to live humble if he changed my name." Changing your name is a kind of initiation. In that case, into the spiritual; one changes one's name in terms of a new spiritual identity, based on the idea of the way names were changed through slavery and, as slaves were moved from one plantation to another, its conceivable they got a new name each time. Then there is the other tradition of nicknames coming along and those names in Afro-American culture, having a greater significance than the names one received from one's parents. I was very alive to that as a kid coming along. This was one of the ways one might reinvent oneself. Reinvention is very important to me as a writer. That is one way in which I think my work is connected to Morrison's and Ellison's, this idea of the reinvention of life, of making one's character in life constantly new, taking what's left over and remaking it into something else and adding a stamp of eloquence and style to that. That style and eloquence is everything. That is so much a part of the culture that black Americans offer which is stunning and new and different. That is the cudgel under which every jazz musician operates.

He had to create anew every night on the set. So this was a part of my growing up, the idea of being alive to change and transformation. The problem is to take this tendency within the culture and to make it new again. So I do not want to take some wonderful, interesting name that I've heard. I have to do something else to it. Maybe link it to other things I'm doing in the novel and to reinvent it again. That is another part of the difference between oral tradition and written tradition. I just don't want to take a name I heard and reecho it in my novel or like Langston Hughes, who takes what he hears and just puts it down that way. I want to take that and remake it again. What helps me to remake it again is my debt and my relationship to traditional literature. I am thinking about what Hardy did with names. So extraordinary with so many wonderful names around me. He's helpful, too in this idea in making a world of the imagination based on a re-creation of reality.

This is also something characteristic of other traditions and other writers, like the Irish, who have faced the same problems. Joyce heard these extraordinary sermons, but he wrote sermons that go beyond what he had heard among the Jesuits. I can't preach with King. I can outwrite him. He wasn't a writer. I can take what he gave me, as a writer and go beyond that. At least I think that is what would make him proud of me, anyway.

# *Divine Days*:
# An Interview with Leon Forrest

Eugene Redmond / 1992

From *Drumvoices Revue* (Fall/Winter 1992/1993). © 1992 by Eugene Redmond.

**Eugene B. Redmond:** Leon, I'm so happy to have you in East Saint Louis, St. Louis, Edwardsville, Fairview Heights, Belleville, Alton. I wanted to start out with a general question. How are you feeling right now about your life, your work as a writer and as an academician? How do you feel about Northwestern, Evanston, Chicago? What's happening right now for you in those arenas?

**Leon Forrest:** Well, hell, I'm waiting on publication of my new novel, *Divine Days*. I hope that it will be well received. That's my main concern right now. And I guess because of the great length of the book, it's 1,135 pages, I'm hoping that reviewers will read some of it before they say this book is too long. But I guess the better reviews will be in the quarterlies where they have time to read. If you write a book this long, if you've got a right mind, then you're really asking whether there are people willing to see how well you sustain character development and so on. It's a lot to ask. Particularly in an age where people don't have that much time for reading. People who do read don't read that much. And then I have a collection of essays. It's coming out next year. And one of them is new. One I recently wrote about Billie Holiday. It's kind of impressionistic. I don't think that it adds anything to the Billie Holiday canon, but it was a lot of fun to write. There are about twenty in there that run a range from Billie Holiday to some literary essays. So that will be out next year.

**EBR:** Do you find the Evanston-Northwestern-Chicago environment a good place to work? Apparently you've produced quite a bit of work there. Are there hindrances of any sort, such as teaching or administration?

**LF:** Well, yeah, there is. And I would predict another generation will probably not go into the university, that writers will do other things. I don't know what

shape that will take. But there are a lot of problems in the general MFA programs where you get people who are talking the same talk, and it means that
young writers get snapped off from getting out into the field, from doing
things like waiting tables, bartending, running with gangs and so on. So
sometimes you get people going from MFA to teaching who've never had any
life experiences. That's one thing that bothers me about a lot of the writing
cadres that you see now. So they talk to each other, but also it drives away
experimental fiction, which is really my interest. You have all this predicted
path of what you must do. I came to Northwestern primarily because the
writers I admired most were back in the university, different from many years
ago. Writers weren't working on newspapers when I was coming alone.
So, I had worked as a journalist for about ten years, and I thought that
the university would be a place where I could grow intellectually, which
would force me to do some close rereading of books to which I had already
been exposed. I was not around long enough to take a degree, so I thought
this would be a way to complete my education. So it's been good in that
sense. It tends to isolate you, but to a degree that's the fault of the writer.
They don't force you to do that. Writing is so lonely, and the hours you
aren't writing you sort of hunger for some immediate kind of conversation
about books. You can't get it in bars. You can get a lot of other things in
bars, but you can't get discussions about books in bars. That's one of the
attractive things about the university. Here's place where you can talk about
books seriously. And there aren't many other places where you can do that
in this society. And that wasn't always true.

**EBR:** This is all very filling. It helps for me personally to flesh out some of
my own views and questions about university life, university work versus
writing, if you want to bring in that kind of contention. I think that we're all
facing it, those of us who work in the university and who also write and do
other things related to writing. You were first established as a journalist.
Could you trace or outline your life up to that point and mention a few of
the things that got you into journalism. Did you work for other publications
besides *Muhammad Speaks*?
**LF:** I had thought that the best way to support myself as I was trying to
write—at first it was poetry, then I got interested in play writing and finally
fiction—was through journalism. I had an interest early on in journalism.
Actually my first job as a journalist was in the army. I was a public information

specialist from 1960 to 1962. I was drafted into the army. I dropped out of college. That was a nice deal. I used to follow troop training and write pieces on
G.I.s with unusual stories. So I did that for about 18 months of my two-year
stint. And then when I came back from the army I continued to work in the family's liquor store. I stopped that after about two years and made a kind of commitment to myself that I was going to go for broke in my writing. Meanwhile, I'd
also secured a job with a small community newspaper, about '65. So I worked
there for three years. I was also editor of the Woodlawn Organization's newspaper. *T.W.O.* is a popular organization in Chicago. And then I left there and went
to work for *Muhammad Speaks* as an associate editor. Meanwhile, I was still writing my fiction in the evening. And I was there at *Muhammad Speaks* from early
1969 through 1973, June of '73. My first book, *There Is a Tree More ancient than
Eden*, was published in May of '73. So I was working on writing fiction while I
was working at *Muhammad Speaks*. One of the nice things about working there
and also at the community papers was that it allowed me a source to get out certain protests or anger. And to look at fiction in a different way when I came
home to write. So that was very healthy. The other thing was that for a long time
on these community papers I was really working about 30 hours a week. It wasn't
a long 48-hour week. So that gave me time too. I wasn't married. I made enough
to support myself minimally. And it allowed me time to write. But all that's part
of the dues paying you have to do. After the novel was published in '73, the
appointment at Northwestern came the same year.

**EBR:** Here's a multi-part question for you. You have now authored, including
this new one, *Divine Days*, four novels, and you speak of some essays. Is there
any way by any stretch of the imagination, that the novels can be seen in a
thematic sequence, possibly a tetralogy? And how much non-fiction have you
written? How much do you plan to write?
**LF:** The non-fiction is more or less occasional pieces put together in this
forthcoming collection of essays. I don't know if I'll write more. But there
seems to be a relationship between a sort of clearing house for essays that
opens you up to possibilities that I haven't talked about in fictional form.
Also, we're dealing with protest, with anger. Also, there's the influence of the
university. I've lectured on this writer and that writer. Ellison and Morrison
and Faulkner. And some of those essays will be in this collection. As for the
sequence of the novels, the first three are a kind of trilogy, though I didn't set
out to plan to do that. It was only until I was deep into the second novel,

*The Bloodworth Orphans*, that I tried to make a continual pattern out of this. The new novel is quite different. There's a lot of comedy in this novel. I hope so anyway. It does take on some of this idea of a kind of mythical area or county. It's very different. It takes place in bars and churches and barber shops. So it's quite different from the other books, even though there are some earlier scenes and characters who come back.

**EBR:** What is the name of your book of essays?
**LF:** The editor offered a title that I'm not that happy about. She wants to call it *The Furious Voice of Freedom*, which seems to me to be something nice if a critic said that, but not for the title of the book. But she likes it, so I'll argue about it. Anyway, it will be out probably in May of next year.

**EBR:** Your answers and observations are providing a lot of insight into writing generally and, of course, for me, the way you work and how you see things. The titles of your books are very intriguing. They're very unusual, very different, startling. In some ways provocative and in some ways, for me, they suggest depth, myth and mythos, image, cosmology, theology, philosophy. When I see the titles, obviously a lot happens for me. What connection is there between the titles and texts? And what connection is there between your various titles? And is there any influence from say, the Nation of Islam or your studies into the theology of Islam under the influence whoever you were in contact with when you were editor of *Muhammad Speaks*? I just keep seeing some connections.
**LF:** Well, it's a good question, because the titles are very intriguing, but I can say that because none of them were my own. That is to say that the titles I had for each of the books originally were probably not good titles. Toni Morrison, who was my editor at the time, said we'll have to get some titles different from these. And it was Toni's suggestion that the title of the first novel be *There Is a Tree More Accident than Eden*. That comes strictly from her. And I gave her the names of about forty titles one weekend and they were all rejected. And she had another title one time too. It was called *Of Eden and Thebes*. That was a title she wanted to call it one time. Then the one I wanted to use was called *Deep Rivers of the Soul*.

**EBR:** Again for Eden.
**LF:** Yes, that's right. So also had many others, but those two come to mind. But finally she suggested *There Is a Tree More Ancient than Eden*, which I really

liked a lot. It seemed too that it was really close to the Negro spiritual "*There is a balm in Gilead.*" It is evocative of so many things that you were mentioning: the crucifixion, the paradise lost kind of thing. So it was a very evocative title, and immediately when she suggested it, I liked it. The next book, I had a title for it too. And she said, "Well, listen, there may be a simpler title." Because you know this is all about the Bloodworth family. So it seemed to me to make sense. So just *The Bloodworth Orphans* was chosen because I wanted to concentrate on that. And since the book itself is long and multi-plotted and there are a lot of different entangled relationships. *Two Wings to Veil My Face*, I forget now what was the original title. I think one was *To Trouble the Waters This Morning.* Morrison didn't care for it that much and I didn't either. She said, "You know, you keep using this song in there, 'Angels got two wings to hide my face. Angels got two wings to fly me away.' " She suggested *Two Wings to Hide My Face*, one of the refrains from this song. I changed it and took the other one, *Two Wings to Veil My Face*, because the veil seemed to be much more poetic, much more elusive, much more suggestive of mask wearing and so on. Then the new book, I was originally going to call—Toni wasn't the editor for this new one—I was going to use the title *The Memoirs of Joubert Jones.* This is his name, the main character, Joubert. After a while that seemed to be a little, well, I tried it on people and people would sort of say, "Well, that's all right." And one of the churches in the novel is called Divine Days and there are other allusions to "Divine Days," so I said I'll try this one and everyone I've mentioned it to has said it's intriguing, this "Divine Days."

**EBR:** That is really informative and exciting. I don't know if I've ever been on such an odyssey before with an author concerning titles. This is one of the most enlightening experiences I've ever had. You and/or Toni came up with those titles, and they are very provocative, and very profound, really. As are your works. The use of myth is very evident, the application of folklore, the use and application of magic, and if I might say, mysticism, ancient things, ancient thoughts and so on. What do you think about myth and folklore and ancient texts? How are you feeling about those as you continue to write, since you apparently rely heavily on what are sometimes called things unknown?
**LF:** Well, some of it has to do with what I've found intriguing in the culture. Again, it's the culture that is the more important source that I seem to be attracted to as a writer. But the source is there and one of the sources is the idea, as you mentioned, of myth. Myth to me is the language attendant to the ritual. And my books are very much about rituals and about anti-rituals. Or

about discovering rituals to sustain life, because one of the great, maybe even gifts, of Black Americans is their ability to reinvent life and make do out of nothing and then put a stamp of style or eloquence upon this reinventive mode. And the myth explains that. The myth reveals that. There's a lot of taboo breaking in Black life, but that's necessary. It's been necessary for us to survive and to put style to it. And style too has to do with myth. Then I guess too I'm attracted to it because of my own background in Catholicism, which really has a mythical quality to it with all the rituals in the Catholic Church and the grand language attended to it. I guess that the South for me has been a kind of mythical home because I don't know the South, but the South comes to me sort of secondhand the way maybe it does with Baldwin in *Go Tell It on the Mountain*. For me, the South is sort of the "Old Country" for African Americans. So that perhaps if I knew it firsthand the way Wright knew it, it would be less awesome, less mythical. It's not mythical when you know that if you walk down that street, that white man's going to shoot you. So to me, in the sense of the lynching and what not, and I would hear a lot about this in my own family, but this was removed from the South here in the North. So it has that quality to it. It seemed to me too that there was always something larger than life in so many of the Black characters that I found I was attracted to or interested in long before I started writing. And these heroes and heroines were oftentimes athletes, sometimes tricksters, sometimes hustlers—often people who seemed to be larger than life with a very complex personality. I never saw enough of that in our fiction, of this complexity. So that was something that really bedeviled me when I began writing fiction, to try to get some of that complexity of Black life into my work. You know, when you talk to people and you say, "That's a complexity," and they say, "Oh, that's not complexity. That nigger's crazy." But looking at it from our perspectives as writers, we say this man is layered, he's moody, he's the thing you hear Black women talking about in bars, "I can't figure him out." That's complexity for the writer. One of the things I'm doing in this new book is a kind of mythical character who's always leaving the scene and coming back with new stories. There's always the story, "Well so-and-so won't be back," or "He's dead." Three months later, well here he appears again. Well that all is mixed up in my imagination with a kind of secular resurrection. He comes back with all these new stories, all these new travels, all these new women he's had, all these new scenes he's seen. There's so much of that, so much ingrained in the Black experience and that's what I've been so attracted to, these larger than life stories. In fact, our story itself is larger than life, if you consider it. And underneath, there's the reading of things that have influenced me like the Bible and Ellison and Faulkner.

**EBR:** Do you find any conflict at all in the multiplicity and the various uses of influences, I mean, across the racial and cultural spectrum? Some writers talk about renouncing or pulling away from influences that are not culturally amenable or culturally similar. I know you mix them in. And whether that's good or great, you accept the influence. Can you say anything at all about that?
**LF:** I'll steal anything I can get my hands on, man, because everything's been stolen from us. And people keep on stepping and making a lot of money off it. I think there are unconscious things that happen in the imagination because long before you start reading you've seen a lot and these things influenced you. But I'm very moved by the Russian writers and I've learned a lot from them. Wherever I can get influence, wherever I can be moved by something, maybe I can use it. To me, it's like if we were surgeons we wouldn't even be talking about this. We would be saying, "Say, you know, the Chinese have made a breakthrough over here. Africans have made a breakthrough over here. I just met this interesting Indian doctor the other day and he told me something about a certain new technique." This is what we're talking about, where I can get new techniques. So I don't have any problem with that at all, but I think a lot of younger people do. Well, it's too bad.

**EBR:** This is very helpful. It places a lot in perspective and helps to frame . . .
**LF:** *I'm* at war with myself on a lot of levels, but that's not a war I'm in, about influences and hang-ups and problems.

**EBR:** You probably addressed this already, but not under the rubric which I am going to suggest it right now. First, do you agree that a good writer or a great writer needs a system of art? I think you outlined something like that a little earlier. And if you do, do you 1) impress this upon writers you train and 2) are you constantly and consciously working out of a system of art?
**LF:** Yeah, I like that term too, because one of the nice advantages I had when I was starting writing rather seriously was that I was involved with the musicians, jazz musicians, painters, academics, and also I was involved with a lot of people who had dropped out of college and were still very interested in reading; films of all kinds, and all of that was useful. So I think that the writer should

be one who nourishes himself of herself in all kinds of other areas of the arts. Certainly, you will be exposed to other writers. That's understandable, but talk to other people in other disciplines. For example, I'm a good friend of Richard Hunt, the sculptor, and sometimes we talk about the process of creativity and it's very enlightening to me because here we do something so different, yet there are a lot of similarities. We believe in work in progress, of leaving something alone and coming back to it, coming back to it with new energies. But again, this goes back to the earlier question you asked about exposing yourself to all kinds of artistic creations. I think the problem for the writer is to develop a rich inner life. That's secret. That's private. What's a rich inner life for me might not be a rich inner life for you. You never know when you talk to a writer. He or she might come on with a big spiel about this or that, but they might not have a rich inner life. Maybe someone over here is rather quiet and may have found the sources to develop a rich inner life. That rich inner life can come from a vast amount of experience, travel, reading, talking to all kinds of people, learning to be a good listener, religion, having a certain stability of home life, having established a certain continuity or pattern of behavior, having a sense of cultural history. All these things you carry within yourself in a certain fragile way that nobody knows about. Learning to develop a secret inner life that's highly contemplative. So all these are source that go into the imagination of the writer.

**EBR:** Again, quite strong and quite full. Stemming or flowing from this idea of an art system, what about mission? Are they one and the same? Are you often conscious of a mission when you're writing? If so, is the mission in the head more that it is in the writing? Is it in the work that's ancillary to writing? Is it in the writing itself? If indeed you see a mission, and I'm thinking of this in the broadest possible context.

**LF:** Yeah, yeah. Well mission isn't a bad word, because there is sense or feeling of a kind of calling after a while. That may sound a little self-serving. But really if you survive a certain amount of time, . . . for example when I look at all the people I knew who wanted to write, but never wrote, or who stopped writing, and somehow I'm still writing, I'm still struggling. That's got to make you feel, "Well maybe there is something, maybe I do have a calling." And then I think the older you get, if you survive that long and have published a little bit, you begin like I do to have a certain responsibility: maybe I've wasted a lot of time, maybe I should even be more cautious with my talent, with my mission as you're saying. And that mission is for me first of all to try to develop my talent the best I can, and I guess a certain level of mission is to try to add to the body of literature of my people and hopefully to influence the national literature. I wouldn't have said that as a younger person, because writing was still sort of fun. I wasn't sure about it. But I do feel through some sense that I've survived this far and, as they say, as certain preachers say, "The Lord wasn't through with me yet."

**EBR:** When you said that you've survived this far, it seemed that there was a silent sigh there and at the same time a silent hurrah. I wonder how a statement that Toni Morrison made sits with you. She said, "The writing is very difficult and very dangerous." We know it's difficult. She said it's very dangerous. She was quoted in *Ebony* magazine, and she has made this statement repeatedly. "Very difficult and very dangerous." Would you concur or cosign that? And how would you embellish it?

**LF:** Well, I don't know concretely what she's talking about, but I would say too that writing is dangerous in the sense that it opens you up to avenues that are not predictable when you first started writing a short story or a novel. Morrison of course is an extraordinarily imaginative writer and writes out of the powers of the imagination and I certainly try to write out of the powers of the imagination. And that means that you don't know where that imagination might take you or what it might unleash within you. And what it unleashes in you might be all kinds of chaos and all kinds of unpredictable and even dangerous perceptions about life and the human condition, race relations, the relationship between men and women; and you wouldn't have predicted it in just normal conversation. The life of the artist is dangerous, and that is why I was talking about just surviving. The artist, maybe even particularly writers, is often time self-destructive. So to try to deal with developing your talent but also deal with your own vulnerabilities and your own weaknesses, that's something to overcome too. Also to have the LUCK to live. You can have the terrible tragedy that happened to your friend [Henry] Dumas. If you have the luck to live and you don't have a terrible illness like Lorraine Hansberry or Frank London Brown or so many talented people like that. If you can survive not drinking yourself to death or dope or sexual vagrancy, all the things that can trap the individual, this means that you've developed a certain kind of toughness. Artists tend to be very destructive, so that you've got to turn those engines over into your creativity, as opposed to those areas of your life that will actually destroy you. That's been a great problem for our great jazz musicians. Charlie Parker, for example, not being able to control that great furor to create. It consumed him.

**EBR:** We are pressing on in our effort to understand literature and the machinations of the mind and the techniques and devices of the writer. I've used the word intrigue quite a bit, but I *am* intrigued by your work and by your life. I'm interested in how you work, the manner in which you work, your use of discipline. I know it's severe discipline, "a very stern discipline," as Ralph Ellison calls it. How do you work? What tools do you use? Do you use longhand, computer, typewriter? Do you work at night, in the mornings? Do you outline stuff and work later? Or do you just use a stream of consciousness thing and then go back and reshape?

**LF:** Well I try to write in the morning, and I find the older I get the better it is to write in the morning. Usually, about 6:30 or 7:00. I'll try to write as long as I can, maybe 'til 11:00, stop, may be do something else, have lunch, and then write if I have the energy, but generally I don't, and I'll probably read in the evening. I find that if you can get three, three and a half, four hours of writing in a day, of intense writing, that's something, because writing takes so much energy. And that energy is not only physical. It's intellectual. And that's different from the painter. A lot of what the painter does is the stroke itself, just filling in spaces. So painters can sometimes paint all day. There's also the fun of painting. Writing is pleasurable. It's not fun to me, I don't think. So it takes a lot of energy to write. It takes a lot of concentration. I usually work from a very general, loose outline, then I'll write a scene over and over again until I get sick of it, then put it away, leave it alone for a long time and then come back to it in maybe two or three weeks or a month later, and then I come to it with a certain kind of coldness, a certain kind of tough-mindedness, I hope. So those are some of the ways I write. Endless rewriting, putting it away and coming back. And another thing for the writer to develop is a sense of living with loneliness, since writing is so lonely. You may be working on something for a long time without showing it to anyone. While if you're a painter, your natural impulse is to have people in to look at what you're doing. Certainly if you're a composer, you'll say, "Here's a tape of something. You can put it in your car and listen to it." But writing seems to be something you've got to sit down and look at, and read, and we don't have that one on one communication with your audience in the way that the other arts do.

And yet, you have to be clever enough as a writer, particularly as a Black artist, to use these other arts. We've accomplished so much in the area of music, of course, and a writer would be foolish not to try to learn a lot about Black music because that's perhaps the art closest to the African American consciousness, at least that's historically been true. Also, the dance is another area we've accomplished so much in, and it's perhaps one of the closest gauges of our consciousness as a people. So the writer needs to be able to draw on those areas of his culture, her culture, where we have accomplished on a very consequent level.

**EBR:** It's quite a scheme, quite a paradigm for how we work as artists generally, as we move down the scale to how the writer works in the overall sense and specifically how you work. W. H. Auden said, "No poem is ever finished. It is only abandoned." How do you know when a work by you is finished for any number of reasons, either you're not going to take it any further, you're not going to show it, or it's ready to be shown or to be published, assuming there is a publisher around? When do you know a work should be abandoned?

**LF:** Well, that does involve a certain amount of risk taking and there's the danger that you might just be exhausted, you as a writer. That's why it's important to put things away and come back to them, and come back with new energies. But maybe more specifically, I can tell with a character when all of the questions I have raised or should have raised about the character and his character in process have been resolved and his energies seem to be spent in the plot. I'm very interested in this novel, *Divine Days*, and I have been since my first novel, in the idea of the character not only in process but also in evolvement, so that it's necessary to put a character through many scenes to draw out all the sides of him or her. So I can usually tell if it [novel] seems to have resolved all of the questions that I can think are demanded of this character in terms of his own quest or the quest of the plot. Now that inherently demands that you put the book away, that you put the manuscript away for a while, and come back and say, "Wait a minute. There's something else demanded of him that I haven't asked and has not been resolved yet." Those are the ways in general in which I feel a sense of closure or completion. In this novel, the new novel, it's so very long and I have so many plots going on, but I have a sense, in reading the galleys anyway, that I have brought into fruition the different plots and brought them into resolution. How successful this resolution is, how eloquent it is, that I don't know. At least I feel relatively comfortable that I've brought all these strands of the plot together.

**EBR:** What do you see down the line? I think of that folk saying immortalized by Baldwin, "I looked down the line and I wondered." Do you look forward to retiring and then writing? And is retiring in the near future? Will you write only fiction and some non-fiction prose? Will you write plays? What's in the future for you as a writer and as a person?
**LF:** Well, I don't think I would think about retiring yet and I still want to teach. As far as writing goes, I want to continue writing novels and more than anything else, that's the dearest. I could see maybe one or two novels already in mind in a general way that I'd like to write. I've kind of enjoyed the two careers, but as we were talking earlier, I'd prefer to have more time to write and perhaps less time to teach.

**EBR:** I think that's a statement that sums up the situation for most of us who are academicians cum writers, or writers cum academicians. Is there a specific project that you are looking at, or is this question too soon behind *Divine Days*?
**LF:** Well, no, I've already started working on something new. And then there was a lot that didn't go into *Divine Days*. There's at least 150 pages I cut from the manuscript. The manuscript was 1,829 pages. And with the cuts and everything, the finished novel is 1,135. But there's a lot that didn't go into it, and I hope to use that in another work. So, there's work to be done. The problem is to find the energy.

**EBR:** I have one last question of you, Leon. I'm most grateful to you and humbled by your great work and the good thinking that has gone in to produce you and all the good stuff around you. Would you indicate by name some of the most indelible influences on your work. Eras, periods, types of writing? Writers? And when you do that, would you also note writers today, kind of star some writers who you feel are doing some things today, whether or not they've influenced you? Who's out there now and what and who is helping to make up what we call American literature, world literature, Black literature, multicultural literature?
**LF:** I guess mainly I've been influenced by what you might call the poets of the novel: Thomas Hardy, William Faulkner, and Ralph Ellison. And then to a

large degree, too, I was influenced earlier by poets. Auden and Dylan Thomas
are among the ones who have really influenced me a lot. And more towards
the recent twenty years, I would say the Russian writers for characterization
and for depth of the human agony and this whole problem of how do you
create a character with these questions of spiritual and political and ideological
anguish. Then, maybe even recently, the Latin American writers like Donoso
and Márquez and Borges. These are writers who create these mythical
worlds. They've also given me a lot of confidence in dealing with my own
Catholicism, since Catholicism is really a minority strand in the Black
American experience. So those are some of the writers who've influenced
me generally over the years. As for contemporary writers, I might not be
as good there. You tend to read certain types of writers you like over again.
But the ones I still admire would be Henry Dumas. I like him. I'm still
interested in so many things he published, and so many things that weren't
published. Morrison of course. The problem too with teaching is that you
tend to reread the books you're teaching over a period of time and you
aren't as adventuresome as you might be. I think what has happened to
me in the last couple of years is that I haven't been doing enough reading
because I've been so consumed with trying to finish this novel. So there
are a lot of new writers I want to read, like [Carl] Phillips and [Terry]
McMillan and [Trey] Ellis. I have found a lot in the work of the stage plays
too of the author of *Ma Rainey's Black Bottom* and *Joe Turner*, August Wilson.
I really like the kind of rowdy power in those scenes of his. Those are some
of the influences. I think more of the influence of individual books than I do
writers. For instance, I certainly don't like all of Faulkner, but a novel like
*Absalom, Absalom!* had a great deal of influence on me. I don't know all of
Thomas Hardy, but I like *Return of the Native* and *Tess of the D'Urbervilles*; and
some of the Russian writers have been very influential. Particularly in doing
long fiction, the Russians are great. Maybe it's those Russian winters; they
don't have anything to do but read. The American writers have not really
stretched out and tried to do big novels, in the sense of the great novels of
the 19th century. I don't know quite why that is. Maybe it's just the impact
of the visual age and people just don't seem to have the time. A lot of
those novels [19th century] were published in newspapers, as scenarios
in newspapers, and newspapers don't do that anymore, hardly. Only
occasionally.

**EBR:** I said that last question would be the last one, but I do have one more, and it's regarding aspiring, developing and emerging writers and your advice to them. What would you, what do you say to writers who are new, not necessarily young because some writers come to the craft in middle age or even in senior age, but what do you have to say to writers aspiring, developing, professional, even mature writers seeking to expand, to probe, to extrapolate those jewels, to mine those fields of experience and other literatures? What do you say?

**LF:** I was laughing at what you're saying because I was in an organization and there was a wealthy woman, and she said she wanted to help young writers, she had just been talking about dancers, these were people 18, 19 years old. We were trying to convince her she wasn't going to get any young writers who publish who are 18, 19. Young writers? We would consider someone in their early '30s young writer. Writers do develop later than the other arts. I would say that anything to develop the imagination, that's your strongest tool. You have to treat it with tender loving care. Read a lot. Get a lot of different varied experiences. That is to say, when you're young, do all kinds of volunteer work in hospitals, in senior citizens homes. That would be a great thing, for instance to read to someone who's blind. Just to read. Try to move away from whatever is the trend. On the other hand, there's always much to be learned from being a bartender or a waiter. Try to find jobs where you aren't drained so that you have time to write when you get home and to read when you get home. If you have a job where you have to bring a lot of work home, that's going to drain you. A young writer has to be willing to make the sacrifices, and those sacrifices are obviously money; and you have to delay a certain level of natural fulfillment. A good thing would be to learn to develop a good ear for listening and to listen to all kinds of conversation. The other things would be to take a good personal assessment of yourself and to find out your weaknesses and your strengths as a person. A lot of times, I would know people who would give away some great lines in bars—they wanted to write, but ended up always writing in the bar, emptying themselves out in the bar. Or maybe someone else has got a problem of running after women. Or somebody else is a heavy drinker. Or another person just doesn't seem to have the discipline. Or maybe another person just doesn't have good health and needs to learn to try to take care of that. It's good to learn and know your strengths and your weaknesses and to learn to work around those. And to develop, if you can, sustain patterns of relationships and friendships. Those are things you borrow on over time. Also, I guess, as a Black writer, to learn the traditions of our people, as I was mentioning earlier, in the dance, in music, as well as in those areas that are strong in the race that you aren't attracted to. For instance, say you're an atheist. That's your business, but you'd better learn something about church, because that's so deep in the history of the race. Also to find the sources that haven't been written about. You were talking earlier about going around and talking with people like the Elks and so on. That's whole area of culture that hasn't been investigated. It behooves the writer to find out about those sources that haven't been investigated that much and to write about them.

**EBR:** Thanks very much, Leon. That was very inclusive. Any writer with his/her wits about him listening to what you just said ought to be able to carry the bacon on in. Leon, you are, among other things, an urban writer. This is not a statement meant to type, of course, but you do work out of an urban setting?—though one would be hard pressed to lack you into any setting since the experiential and experimental, seem to work quite well, almost interchangeably, interdependently and interrelatedly in your work. What do you think about these cities, the struggle in these cities, the people in these cities, the art in these cities, the language in these cities? What are your thoughts about cities? Cities dying? Cities living? Cities coming back? Cities fading?
**LF:** Well, I guess I was going to say too at the end of the things to the writer, that maybe the Black writer needs to find out his or her relationship to other ethnic groups. Just as we are much concerned now with our relationship with Africa and our African past, we need to know our relationship to the growing Hispanic population. The dwindling, but still very powerful, white population, white ethnics in the city. Then how can that be translated into political authority and might. And to try to find some new techniques for survival. Because you go to these conferences, and always the theme is "Where do we go from here?" That's been going on since Malcolm died. So, nobody has any new answers. One of the things I did like about the civil rights movement was that at least people were addressing techniques for how to deal with white power. Now all we need is bright people to come along with new techniques for how to deal with our problems in the cities. I guess, from a perspective of people like ourselves, it would certainly have to do with the importance of reading, of course, because we've got to see that it is one of the tools we've got to use to help free ourselves. So massive programs to bring in

reading, almost to force young people to read, and to see that this is an important part of our liberation. That's one thing. Maybe, to approach this problem with great humility and say, "Well, look, you know, best I talk about reading and writing since that's the only thing I've proven I could do. I cannot tell you about government or anything else." Try to have people to bring in their expertise in a specific way, rather than these people who get up and give you this great sermon on our problems and in the meanwhile ain't told you nothing new.

**EBR:** Thank you, again, for observations on the city, survival and struggle, possible innovative looks and approaches to uplift and self-reliance, multiculturalism and so forth.

# The Mythic City:
# An Interview with Leon Forrest
Kenneth W. Warren / 1992

From *Callaloo* 16:2 (1993), 392–408. © Charles H. Rowell. Reprinted with permission of The Johns Hopkins University Press.

**Warren:** Your most recent novel, *Divine Days*, entangles your reader in a web of family relations. Perhaps talking about your family might be a good place to begin. In an autobiographical essay you have written that you were "raised by a magical seamstress, a lady who was always transforming life: first, the cloth, now the body and then the very spirit of the recreated person before our eyes." Can you tell us a little more about being raised by your Aunt Lenora Bell and how it has shaped your approach to writing novels?
**Forrest:** She was actually a part of the extended family really. She wasn't related to us, but had raised my mother and was very instrumental in my raising and rearing. She was a complicated woman, a Republican—one of the very few Republicans around the neighborhood. She was also quite a good storyteller and would read to me a lot. And then, as I said in my article, she had all of these patterns in her room of works she was designing and dresses she was interested in making. So, it was very interesting for me to have a person who was not related in a direct way and yet was very much interested in being a kind of matriarch, I suppose, in the family . . . and to have someone who was serious about reading to talk to in my formative years.

**Warren:** So you say she was a storyteller. What kind of stories . . . ?
**Forrest:** She would talk about growing up in Kentucky and her family. One brother had owned, as she says, a saloon (she was very refined), and the other brother died when he was quite young. And then her mother, who was a mulatto, was part of a group of teachers in Kentucky. So she was not that far really from slavery. And then my great-grandmother on my father's side—was born in 1875, and her mother had been in slavery. And so even though I was born in 1937, I wasn't that far from some of the stories that

were either near slavery or at the frontier of it. And that's perhaps one of the reasons why I got interested in trying to write novels that had an historical sweep to them . . . but in a mythical sense . . . since I wasn't there nor were the people who I talked to really in the slave experience, but they knew of it.

**Warren:** OK . . . so then, were there other storytellers? Your fiction is populated by people who are always somehow telling their narratives and interweaving their various stories.
**Forrest:** I mentioned, too, a great-uncle of mine who went to school with Louis Armstrong in New Orleans—George Dewey White who was quite a storyteller and a barber. And as you were sitting their getting your hair cut, he would tell you stories. He was always renaming people in the family. In families generally at this time, kids didn't talk very much. So you would just sit there and listen, you know, and you'd better not speak out too much. But it worked well because it allowed me to develop this layered sense of storytelling from various voices . . . and yet to keep them separate. My mother's side of the family was completely different from my father's side of the family. And then there was this Aunt Bell who was not related by blood but had raised my mother and me. And that was interesting just in terms of getting these separate sides of the family straight. Now I tried to incorporate in terms of my own fiction the sense of the diversity of the group. So that perhaps helped me a lot when I first started writing, to have that kind of background where these voices were very separate.

**Warren:** Now the separate sides of the family . . . do they correspond to the differences, say, in the Catholicism on the one side and the Protestantism on the other?
**Forrest:** That's right.

**Warren:** It's relatively unusual in the African American experience that you get a representation of Catholicism as a force. Can you talk a little bit more about how Catholicism and African American literature and life come together for you?
**Forrest:** Well, it was very hard because of the Catholic church at that time seemed to be so far from the ethos of African Americans. Whereas if I was in Haiti, a Haitian writer, it would have been wonderful. Instead, it was just another way in which it seemed to me my own background was so splintered

that I would never be able to write anything. A Catholic on one side . . . a Protestant on the other. And there are all kinds of other divisions within divisions. But reading Joyce and also later reading the Latin American writers gave me a certain confidence in using the Catholic experience, simply because that was their experience—the Catholic Church—and they obviously wrote out of it with a certain strength and robustness. But it also gave me a confidence that I could use it in a way. And so that was one thing, but was a long time coming. I think I was more influenced by the ritual of the Catholic Church.

Then with the Protestants I was more influenced by the spirituals, in particular the gospels and preaching, because I didn't go to a Catholic school, which was different from all my cousins. They all went to Catholic school and were sufficiently indoctrinated. I had the blessing of going to a black school with some very powerful and prideful black teachers. So I learned some Negro history. And then we also sang spirituals and so on. From my father's side of the family I began to get a sense of the importance of the folk preacher. It seems to me that has saved my artistic life, really. I never would have made that discovery if I had only gone to the Catholic church—Catholic school.

**Warren:** In what way did it save your artistic life?

**Forrest:** Because it gave me the voice into the conscience of the race. And I feel the preacher is really the bard of the race. And the church is also the place where the highest level of eloquence is projected—at least that was true when I was a kid. It's the place that even then made the connection between the spiritual and the secular experience . . . the spiritual and the political experience.

**Warren:** So you see that the folk tradition as it came up from the South to the urban centers of the North managed to sustain itself and did not, as writers, say, from Jean Toomer and Richard Wright suggest, tend to die out because it didn't provide the kind of sustaining force that . . .

**Forrest:** Oh, yes, I think so. In Chicago and many other urban centers it still flourished. And witness even today the tremendous amount of powerful preaching in different black pulpits every Sunday in Chicago. And a lot of that is still southern preaching to a large degree—structurally and oratorically and so on. Now that also has to do with the fact that in my own fiction anyway there's a much more celebratory fervor, I think, than you get with some of the realism school.

**Warren:** That's what's fascinating about your work. Chicago has certainly figured into American literature for well over a century now, but it seems to call forth a realistic ethos in writers whether you're talking about Theodore Dreiser, Frank Norris, or Richard Wright. Why does it strike a mythic chord in you?

**Forrest:** Well, mythic and comic in its resiliency. It's a city of a hustler. It's a city where you can get knocked down and smashed and make a comeback. I mean within the black community. Because it is a hustler's town and because it was said that if you came to Chicago you could get a job. In fact, these were the papers sent South—*The Defender, The Courier*—"Come to Chicago for a job!" And that kind of life, you know was really the nourishing form in my own background coming up in the '40s and '50s. It was only later that a lot of that began to break down. But even then it was a city for the hustler. And that was the difference from many other cities—Cincinnati, Cleveland, different places—where if you were to get into public trouble or corruption you can't make a comeback. But in Chicago . . . just lay low awhile and you can come back.

**Warren:** So does that explain why the folk preacher and the hustler are not so very far apart?

**Forrest:** Well, that's right . . . that's right. And of course the trickster of many kinds.

**Warren:** Say more about the role of the trickster in your work.

**Forrest:** The trickster, to me, is the one who is not an agent of healing as it is in the African tradition where with the magical gods the story is ultimately worked out and harmony is brought forth. Rather a trickster is one who is always manipulating chaos for his own good and cunning, and there are all kinds. I mean there is the kind who is trickster as demon, that I deal with a little bit in *Divine Days*. And one of the things that I was trying to get at in *Divine Days* with the character Sugar-Groove, who is out of a trickster as hipster perhaps, is this other side of him that begins to turn a lot in the latter part of his life towards generous works and also apparently goes through some kind of spiritual metamorphosis.

**Warren:** So this trickster, and we can keep Sugar-Groove in mind here, do you see it as specific to African American literary tradition, or is he something like the conman that we see cropping up in most American literature?

**Forrest:** He would be both, of course. He is an American, so that is certainly part of the terrain. But it's increased for blacks because so much of what was available to make a living after the height of the job openings for blacks in the '40s and '50s and early '60s had to do with a kind of underground economy. And that underground economy sometimes was something like, for instance, a person who might be a numbers runner, or maybe an ambulance chaser, to someone on the other end of the spectrum who might be running drugs. But so much of what was available had to do with a coming up with a cunning hustle . . . a device . . . a certain kind of hustle to survive. And inherent in that was the role of the trickster.

**Warren:** So does that describe the writer as well?

**Forrest:** The writer is taking a tremendous gamble in whatever he or she is working on. That it will all come out. And if you're ambitious enough you're rolling dice with some pretty rugged people who are no longer around, but their books are there to outwit.

**Warren:** So those rugged people include Joyce, Faulkner, Ellison. Talk about how you see yourself in relation to any particular literary tradition.

**Forrest:** I see myself in line in at least three traditions. One would be the very specific tradition of Langston Hughes and Sterling Brown—writers who used oral tradition and to a certain degree extended it a bit in their poetry. And then in a larger tradition with Ellison and Hayden—writers, I think, who took the oral tradition and recombined it with Western intellectual traditions, literary traditions, and placed yet a higher stamp upon their art. Then there was their connection with the larger American traditions of Poe and Faulkner and Melville and so on (the connections between Ellison and Melville, as you know, are very keen). That's another connection. And then ultimately, of course, the connection that we all have as American writers to the best achievements in the novel form of the 19th century as we've seen through European literature and Russian literature. So those are about three or four connections I like to make. I mean, I have been very much influenced by a lot of the writings later in Dostoevsky—in particular those wonderful monologues in *Crime and Punishment* and the *Brothers K.* and the investigation of this kind of tormented inner soul, and the idea that a guy can come in a tavern and tell you his story and that story in itself is an odyssey. Well, that's very different from what we had many hundreds of years ago where the only person who would have these extraordinary stories would be the world travelers. Here a person can live a life in a city and have an odyssey. And that connects us to, of course, obviously with both Dostoevsky, and of course, particularly with Joyce whom we were talking about.

**Warren:** OK . . . this brings up a number of questions. One comes from the fact that along with writing you also teach literature, specifically, African American literature. Do you find that students are receptive to the idea that they ought to have read Dostoevsky and Joyce in order to understand, say, what Ellison is up to and indeed, what you are up to—your fiction?
**Forrest:** No, because students, whether it's a literature class or a creative writing class, want to assume that literature is original in a way that nothing is original. I sometimes talk about all the influences in Morrison's work—and they're all over the place as they are with any first-rate writer—because she was very well read before she ever started thinking about writing. But students tend to feel that it dampers originality, the creativity of a writer, for you to point this out too much. Or others will feel rather intimidated by it.

**Warren:** Do they respond differently if the influences you allude to are other African American artists say, rather than Russian or Irish?
**Forrest:** Yes, somewhat. Then there's the question of gender, too, because if you mention some male figure—well, "Why not just other women?" I'm always anxious to point out, "Yes, but they're taking on men on what was supposedly only male grounds and in many cases outdoing them." But this gets into the ambitions of the writer. So unless it's an advanced class, it's like that wonderful Melville story—they "prefer not to."

**Warren:** Well, you've mentioned the two words, tradition and then the ambitions of the writer, which suggests that one's attitude toward tradition is certainly not a matter of simple reverence. That is, when you sit down to write a novel, you're not approaching these great figures as simply icons; you're engaged in some sort of battle.
**Forrest:** The first expression is reverence, of course, when you read them when you're very young. The second is to think about, "Now, how can I cut my own path around this lion or lioness, or conversely, take him or her on in areas that they didn't know that well, but only suggested." That's certainly been my

relationship with Faulkner about the folk preacher. Because I was very much taken with that wonderful little sermon of Reverend Shegog's in *The Sound and the Fury*, but I soon enough figured out that, hell, I'd know more about black sermons than Faulkner did. And why shouldn't I after all? I still salute him for doing that fine sermon and I wish others would have tried to do it. A lot of times a writer, an older writer, a prominent or famous writer, can suggest some clues for you to try to broaden or expand that he or she only touched upon.

**Warren:** So then, in your attitude toward these older writers, two of the key words that come up again in your own discussions about your fiction and the discussion the critics are engaged in about your fiction are transformation and reinvention. Can you elaborate on these words?
**Forrest:** Transformation always refers to character and the idea that the kinds of black characters I'm interested in, the major ones anyway, are often going through several stages of psychological, spiritual, and political transformation. Sometimes in terms of strength and sometimes in terms of destruction, which is in *Divine Days* both with Sugar-Groove and also Imani. Reinvention seems to me so much a part of the black ethos, of taking something that is available or maybe conversely, denied blacks and making it into something else for survival and then adding a kind of stamp and style and elegance. And it's all through African-American music and jazz and it's obviously all through sports of all kinds, and I think it's the link I have to Morrison and to Ellison. It's something a lot of the Afrocentric people haven't seen . . . that we're not simply a repository nor a reflection of the African experience, but that we're constantly remaking everything that was left over from Africa, everything that we got from the Europeans, into something completely new that both the Africans couldn't do and the Europeans couldn't do. Europeans didn't create jazz and neither did the Africans. Black Americans did that.

**Warren:** How then do you account for the popularity of Afrocentrism . . . ?
**Forrest:** It's part of our search—the African American search—for wholeness and, also in some cases, for a purer answer.

**Warren:** Now you're moving toward some of the more obvious, say, political import of reinvention in your works as well. Do you see that your work is engaging in contemporary political debate in any particular way?
**Forrest:** Maybe the last novel *Divine Days* does. But it seemed to me the way to approach that was through some satire and comedy in a way. Because one

of the problems with much of the contemporary arts that I've seen is that they have these sort of easy pat answers. For instance, at the end of this play, between Malcolm X and Martin Luther King, there is this embrace, and now they're brothers, you know, which is really so much bullshit. Because what this resolution does is to narrow the toughness of the individual arguments that these men had with each other and about society. And this was serious business on the part of both men that they really believed in what they were doing and that the other fellow was going the wrong way. But I've noticed this with a number of recent, well-thought-of pieces, whether movies or novels in which some sort of easy embrace is forged and that in doing that it doesn't strengthen the group, but it suggests a kind of pabulum.

**Warren:** Do you see that going on with students you're teaching here at Northwestern?
**Forrest:** Well, to the degree that they segregate themselves from the larger campus . . . yeah. This, of course, has to do with several reasons. One is that many come from the black middle and upper-middle class growing in the cities quite strong and very insular, with little experience of harmony with whites and little reason to feel that they would be integrated. The other part is the understandable pride of a people on the way up. And then, of course, all of the vicious racism that has been visited on these campuses in the last five years or so . . . so a lot of that has to do with this will to segregate.

**Warren:** Well, it sounds like a climate where satire and parody would be a risky venture.
**Forrest:** Well, I haven't written any novels about Northwestern. . . .

**Warren:** But if we take Northwestern as something of a microcosm . . . of a larger moment. . . .
**Forrest:** Well, there's a need for it, I think, because satire and comedy force you to divest yourself of your pomposity about your own demonically held vision, you know. And it also helps you laugh at yourself and it means that the individual has to come up with a tough-minded approach to life, so it can be very useful.

**Warren:** I'm thinking here of the moment in *Divine Days* where Joubert Jones is speculating on the possibilities of dramatizing the outlandish exploits of the Black Muslim Leroy 5X Jones, and he ends up worrying on the one hand that he could be accused of being an Uncle Tom on the one hand and on the other an anti-Semite. . . .

**Forrest:** Oh, yes . . . that's a small scene. But what's happened is really like a fairy tale—a truck capsizes on the freeway, and all these pigs are running around. The Muslim, who's gone in and out of the Nation, grabs one and is barbecuing. Joubert is thinking about taking a creative writing class, and he says that maybe he might write about it, but then he would run into some of the problems, you know . . . as you're talking about, about how students would accept this guy eating pork—Muslim and Jewish kids—would not accept that. So it is a problem of how people will accept humor—if they will use it as a way of purgation and as a way of self-cleansing and coming clean with themselves and their society. But if you present these romantic images that are so false to human feeling and ideology, then you do literature and you do the group harm.

**Warren:** Well, then what's interesting about the year 1992 is we have the publication of *Divine Days* and then, much later in the year, we have the release of Spike Lee's film on Malcolm X. Now, one might describe the film as a canonization of Malcolm X as a quintessential black male hero toward whom the ideal posture is one of reverence. And yet, you have a novel here that takes an irreverent stance towards heroism. One of the epigraphs with which you begin the text is a quote from Joyce in which he says the "whole structure of heroism is and always will be a damned lie." And later on you have a character who speaks very disparagingly of "Malcolm-mania." What are your feelings toward the contemporary reception of Malcolm X, either through Spike Lee's film or just a general attitude towards him as a historical figure?

**Forrest:** Well, I think that he is attractive because he represents opposite ends of the spectrum here. One, that he was such a consummate hustler and almost eventually as demon, but was successful in that world. Then he had the pins kicked out from under him and went through this spiritual metamorphosis in jail. And then he epitomized the other end of it, and that is the great potential of leadership. And that leadership represented the ability to tell whites off, and also to tell off the subservient black leadership. So all of that is quite attractive, and the odyssey of it is attractive. But what is missed here is any sort of criticism of Malcolm the person. The tendency is to deify two forms of figures, one, the underground hero, and then the hero who, when he was with the

Muslims, even there he was a hero who was not accepted by the larger reaches of black society, nor whites. Though there's every reason for him to be the kind of yeasty mythical figure—you know, he's only been dead thirty years—that people would revere now, because he's almost like a grandfather figure to many of the young kids; it's almost been that far away from them. Then the other point is that you've got a lot of other people who would be in their mid-'40s or maybe even older who are in important positions now, and for them Malcolm was an extraordinary hero when they were growing up. Now they're in the position of writing and expressing themselves, or in powerful situations, and they want a rethinking of Malcolm. Many of them have had the problem of running into what we would call, I guess, the glass ceiling in their own professional careers . . . and say, well, maybe Martin was wrong . . . maybe Malcolm was right . . . about the limits of society.

**Warren:** Does his career still strike you as a career of possibility in terms of the present moment . . . and how one reinvents Malcolm X?
**Forrest:** Yes, but he is full of reinvention . . . I'm fearful that not enough is given to the process of that reinvention—that was my point—through the Muslims, for instance . . . that really made his life. And then, of course, there is all of the naivete of Malcolm, and the gullibility of him with *The Messenger*. I mean anybody who knows anything about preachers and is surprised that this preacher had an adulterous life has got to be pretty naive. But it's a fascinating story and it should be looked at more as a kind of saga as opposed to holding fast to everything that he said or did in his public life, because he was constantly making a lot of mistakes. He made mistakes in terms of his ability to access Elijah. He made mistakes certainly in his relationship with the civil rights movement . . . and he really apparently wanted in there. He certainly was a poor leader in terms of organizing people. What he could do was get a lot of people interested in what he was saying, but the kind of organization that you need to undergird a leader, that wasn't his strength. That was more of the precinct captain's strength that Elijah had.

**Warren:** You said he made mistakes in regard to the Civil Rights Movement. Are you talking about his early uncompromising posture?
**Forrest:** I think he wanted the Muslims to move in that arena. Not only civil rights, but particularly the Freedom Movement aspect of the Civil Rights Movement . . . and the political arena . . . and he couldn't get them to do it.

**Warren:** Well, your early career also includes a year as managing editor of *Muhammad Speaks*. How does that figure into your view, both of say, the Muslims or Malcolm X, or even your own work today?

**Forrest:** I thought quite highly of them on certain levels. One of them is the self-help business, which we still need. You look in the slums, there is a desperate need for some of these Mom and Pop stores, and even the Your Supermarkets. The racism in the faith was dangerous and unfortunate, although I must say that for the people they were dealing with, who were so dead spiritually, you needed something of a shock treatment, sort of an electric shock to awaken this dead man. And some of that shock had to be spiritual and nationalistic. Now, the problem is when the nationalism veers over into racism. Then when that happens obviously, it does all kinds of damage to the people who are on the way up. It cuts them off from the intellectual resources that they need. "Well, after all, whites are doing this, we don't need that; Asians are doing this, we don't need that." And after a while, you're into another kind of segregated hold.

**Warren:** But is there something in nationalism that makes that kind of turn inevitable?

**Forrest:** Not necessarily at all. The Irish in Chicago, and in many places in this country really, the fervor that went into their political rise was nationalistic. But then you've got to turn the corner and let that nationalism and self-pride open you up to the larger resources of the outer society. It doesn't have to turn into racism. As a matter of fact, a lot of the people who are very popular or well-known—Powell for one and probably Mayor Washington—were initially nationalists, but along the way they are able to mix in other ingredients into their personality development. And one thing that can do that, of course, is to increase one's reading so that you're not just reading only *The Message to the Black Man* a hundred times, but you're reading a larger library and learning the techniques of political savvy that individuals from other groups have tried.

**Warren:** Well it sounds, then, as if the Chicago political machine was one place in the past in which this kind of reinvention or crossing of boundaries actually took place . . . that you perceive something positive in that old. . . .

**Forrest:** Well, I see something positive in the sense that it gave people an experience. And a lot of people that broke with the machine initially were benefited by the machine in terms of learning politics. Then they had something to break with. But if you don't have anything to break with, then you don't have anything, you know. So that silent six or eight aldermen that Washington eventually had to fight with, too—even Washington himself—also came out of the machine at one time. But at least it gave people a grounding. The Muslims, of course, were enormously conservative. And still are. Malcolm was able to get himself together by going through this kind of conservative mode and then eventually making a kind of radical break with them.

**Warren:** You also worked with community newspapers. How did that help shape your vision as a writer?

**Forrest:** I was with The Woodlawn Organization's newspaper, *The Observer*. I was editor there for a time. It was really good because it allowed me to get out a certain kind of first heat about the political situation—poverty and race and so on. And I could come to my fiction, when I would work on it in the evenings, looking at a literary life in a different way, in an imaginative way. Whereas I think what happened to a lot of people in the late '60s and early '70s is that they got their politics and ideology mixed up with their poverty and their fiction. So it was good in a cunning sense. It was also good training in terms of interviewing people, in terms of learning what could make a story, a certain compactness of language. And it also helped train me to write at the typewriter. So those years were very good. There was also something that got involved in my personality for a long time: the idea of having many different lives. So I guess I've always been attracted to people like that, and have tried to capture characters like that in my novels, who suffer from something more complicated than double-consciousness.

**Warren:** Multi-voiced.

**Forrest:** Multi-souled.

**Warren:** Which described the plight of Joubert Jones in many respects.

**Forrest:** Yeah, I guess so.

**Warren:** Who was also a journalist.

**Forrest:** He's a bartender, though.

**Warren:** Now people have mentioned what they see as the autobiographical aspects of *Divine Days*. Did you conceive this as an autobiographical novel?

**Forrest:** Well, no, I didn't. But my God . . . we're talking about a manuscript that was 1,829 pages. I wouldn't have an autobiography that could go on that long. But on the other hand, I'll use anything I can get my hands on if I can use it in an imaginative way. And there are many things that have happened to me that I can't write about. They don't do anything for the imagination. But I might hear a story that you would tell me about something that happened to you that would just take me away, and the imagination would soar with it. So I'm always looking at the resources that can go into developing a rich inner life. And that hopefully enriched inner life can act as a springboard for the agency of my imagination. That's always what I'm looking at. Well, a lot of things that have happened are so intimate and I wouldn't mind writing about them, but I just don't seem to have any will over them, or power over them. I have encountered people in my life who were so powerful. I've tried to write about them, but I'm still overpowered by them.

**Warren:** So you keep at that?
**Forrest:** Well, I don't because I go not to something or someone that maybe I've only known quite peripherally but that encounter unleashed perhaps the characterological makeup within me of a certain character, a certain kind of character, who has been there for a long time, brooding.

**Warren:** So clearly the novel is your preferred form, but Joubert is a would-be playwright. Why is he a playwright? Why are you a novelist? What effect does form have on vision?
**Forrest:** Well, we don't know if Joubert is ever able to find the form. He's writing out in longhand this story of Sugar-Groove, and he hopes to convert that into a play. And of course he has written a play on Ford. So it seems to me my distance in relation to Joubert is that I have published novels and I am writing this novel that was published in *Divine Days*, and he's at perhaps an earlier stage in his development let's say. So, that was one kind of thing. Some of the things he encounters I have encountered and others not. I certainly don't hear all these voices that he hears. He's always hearing voices.

**Warren:** So were you attracted to other forms? I know you've written a libretto.
**Forrest:** I wanted to write poetry for a long time, but I couldn't get command of the eloquence of poetry and the form of it. I had all these poets that I admired so much, that were so grand and I couldn't equal that. But I kept

some of that love of language alive, and also the idea of rewriting endlessly the way poets do. For a long time Dylan Thomas was a favorite of mine. Thomas had this method of working where he would change one word of a poem and then would rewrite in longhand the whole poem out . . . particularly the major poems like "Fern Hill" and "The Ballad of the Long-Legged Bait" and the sonnets. He left behind over 225 working papers. So some of that carried over into my obsessive rewriting of fiction. And obviously the love for language. But the discipline of poetry at its highest level seems to me still the consummate literary art.

**Warren:** Do you think at some point you will go back?
**Forrest:** Occasionally, I'll write a little poem on a sort of ceremonial event. So many of the people in *Divine Days* are writers of one kind or another. Aunt Eloise is a newspaperwoman, and Joubert. And there's the guy that runs around the tavern all the time . . . Nightingale. Joubert's grand-uncle writes poetry. So there's some others searching for voices.

**Warren:** Searching for forms as well.
**Forrest:** Imani has a brother who's a playwright.

**Warren:** Now you suggested that for you one of the legacies of having been writing for community newspapers in the '60s was a discipline and an awareness of the need to distinguish what you were doing as journalist and what you were doing as a novelist. But you also suggested that others weren't as successful as you at seeing the apparent pitfalls, as you say, of not being able to distinguish between the two. What do you feel is the legacy of the '60s in terms of African American literary achievement today? Do you see something positive having come out of, say, the Black Arts Movement? The Black Aesthetic?
**Forrest:** Well, when you think about the writers who have really made the big thrust in African American literature, they really start about 1970, I'd say, with *The Bluest Eye*. Beginning maybe with McPherson's stories in '69. McPherson, Wideman, Morrison, Walker—you can just go on and on—Gaines. These were writers who were really not touched directly by the Black Arts Movement. And that's sort of a story in itself. In fact, many of them wouldn't have been all that welcomed by the Black Arts Movement.

**Warren:** But could one argue that the mere presence of the movement itself gave them something to work against? Or that the battle that those writers were fighting during the '60s somehow enabled the success that you begin to chart in the 1970s?

**Forrest:** Perhaps so. I mean, that would be the work of the scholar. But the published works of Gaines and Walker are really quite different from the Black Arts Movement. The works were so well-written that they were incorporated into magazines like *Negro Digest* and so on. But really they were doing something quite different. Toni, of course, would be old enough to certainly have witnessed the Black Arts Movement. But even then she was working on *The Bluest Eye*. But *The Bluest Eye* wouldn't have any place in the Black Arts Movement. You'd have to go down the line, I guess, and look at the particular writers and what they were publishing during that time and see how much of it was really, in fact, stuff out of the ideology of the Black Arts Movement. I certainly know that I can't think of one novel of any particular strength that emerged out of the Black Arts Movement.

**Warren:** What about poetry?

**Forrest:** Poetry all over the place, and then the question is, "Well, how strong is the poetry?" There certainly was a lot of energy and there was also activity, to a degree, in the theater. But I think one of the legacies would be the energy that comes out of the Black Arts Movement, best revealed in poetry. Some poets have emerged. It seems to me you have to go in stages a little bit, like the Beat period. Well, who are the writers who emerged out of the Beat period? There aren't that many when you think about it. It was primarily a white movement with the exception of Baraka. So it isn't just putting a bad mouth on Black Arts, but just any movement. How many survive out of that? And there aren't that many given the great numbers who were involved in the Black Arts Movement. In Chicago, I think of Sterling Plumpp, but Sterling has gone on because he got reinvolved with the blues idiom, which has really saved him as a poet. And you know there are others who have been able to recombine the energy of the Black Arts Movement with the Women's Movement, for instance, like Sanchez and Evans and some of the others. But if these writers didn't recombine that energy with other energies then, by and large, they lost. They lost out because that was the first kind of feverish energy of a young creativity. And if that isn't recombined with other strengths either out of the culture or literary traditions, then the writers have fallen by the wayside. And that always happens.

**Warren:** Now you chair the African-American Studies department here at Northwestern. Could one say that the true legacy of what was going on in the '60s with the Black Arts Movement was precisely the movement of African American studies into the academy and the institutionalization of African American studies? Does that strike you as accurate?

**Forrest:** It certainly had some impact, there's no doubt about that. First of all around maybe '66, '67, many schools started opening up a bit and then as you know, of course, after Dr. King's death there was a tremendous sense of guilt in all these universities about a lot of things. And the black students were able to say, "Well, you know, we're uncomfortable here and a lot of it has to do with the black or African experience." And so it had a kind of historical sweep to it. To bring in everything back from Martin Delany or, even before that, everything African in to the canon or into what was being taught. And they were probably energized a lot by what you're saying about reading Sanchez and many of the poets. But their great interest was to bring in the whole sweep of denied intellectual resources, I think. There's certainly a lot to what you're saying and a lot of their direct heroes would have been women and men who were in the Black Arts Movement. That's for sure.

**Warren:** Do you think that the future—as an administrator of an African-American Studies program—do you think that the future of these programs is bright? Or dim?

**Forrest:** Well, I think it's going to be very useful for universities because of the demographics at the turn of the century where you have many more people of color in the university who want to go to the sources of ethnicity. On the other hand, most of our class is, $\frac{2}{3}$ of the students who take our classes are white. So yeah, I think it's here to stay . . . and, of course, students generally want to take something about the black experience simply because you can't go through a three-month period without something extraordinary happening to black people in a large sense in this society, as revealed in the news. And people want to know about it, whether it's Rodney King one month and Malcolm X the next, you know. And so on. And students generally want to have some sense of what that means.

**Warren:** Does that put pressure on the African American courses to be. . . .

**Forrest:** Topical . . . yes. It sure does. And the problem is, as I was mentioning earlier, is to connect up with the larger historical background. So if you're going to talk about Malcolm, talk about Nationalism, and then you're back to Martin Delany, or you're going through Garvey and Delany and so on. But try to give them some sense of the sweep of everything that seems to be most immediate. If you're talking about Rodney King, well, that gets us back to Richard Wright, in the South, and to Faulkner and the writers who talked about the degradation of blacks through the police state. . . .

**Warren:** Let's switch gears for a moment and go back to your career as a novelist. How would you describe your trajectory beginning with, say, *There is a Tree*, and ending up most recently with *Divine Days*. Do you see yourself charting a particular course as a writer or is it more serendipitous in terms of what comes next?

**Forrest:** It is open-ended in a sense of what might come next because I'm always working on little patches here and there. Little stories. I'll work on half-a-dozen pages or so and then I'll put them aside and come back and rewrite them endlessly and try to forget about them. So later I can come back to them with a certain tough, cold eye, let's say. I never know where things are going. I don't use much of an outline. I work from a very vague outline and I improvise that like a jazz musician over and over again. On the other hand, it is by now apparent to me that there is a little mythical kingdom (not an original thought) that I've been developing and so I am very much concerned with trying to bring certain areas into it that I haven't written about before.

**Warren:** Do you see yourself staying in the boundaries of Forest County as you look forward to your next work?

**Forrest:** Yeah, I think so because I might as well. I don't have that much time left. So I, you know, better do what I can do the best. And there's so many things I can't do in terms of writing, and there are certain things I can do and so I suppose I'd best stick to what I can do.

**Warren:** Would you want to talk a little about what you think is coming up next . . . ?

**Forrest:** There was a lot left over from, believe it or not, *Divine Days*. There were about 150 pages cut from it and a long scene in there it seemed to me that I could just cut out and save. And that's a scene with Joubert in the army. I'm going to use that and that should be pretty interesting. And there were several sections of work that I wanted to use in *Divine Days*, and that might be another novel, a kind of sequel, but I never know if I can energize it. That's my problem.

**Warren:** And how do you discover that moment when you energize it?
**Forrest:** Through hard work and rewriting over and over again. And you know, maybe I'll hit something that will just . . . the juice will shoot through it. And then I'm on the way to agony and ecstasy or something. But I don't know if that's going to happen. And then there's another one that would take up the life of Nathaniel around the time he's 14. I have a lot of that manuscript, in fact. This was really a love story about a woman who commits suicide, and it's told in voices: several people trying to get a handle on why she commits suicide. I abandoned that because, at the time, I didn't think I had the power or control or whatever it takes to finish so then I got working upon the idea of *Two Wings to Veil My Face*.

**Warren:** So this is something you've been thinking about coming back to then . . . ?
**Forrest:** Yeah, that's right. So those are two kinds of projects. And then there's another one which might be a series of short stories. And so there are all these little dribbles and patches around. Maybe I can forge them into a story. I also have a collection of essays coming out next year, as you know.

**Warren:** Coming out early next year?
**Forrest:** They'll be out in about May. One of them is a long essay on Billie Holiday . . . which, I think, is going to be in this special issue of *Callaloo*.

**Warren:** Well, since you've brought up Billie Holiday . . . talk a little bit more about her as a major facet of your aesthetic . . . her voice is referred to often.
**Forrest:** I suppose she was more powerful than even I realized. My mother loved her a lot and really seemed to have understood her art quite a bit . . . used to play her songs a lot and would point to things that she thought she was doing. And she was about the same age (well, she was a bit older than my mother) but we used to listen to her all the time. I became intrigued more and more on my own with her because it seemed to me that she was a good example of the artist as thinker. And then all the problems of life that she had to contend with, she was able to turn them into this haunting artistic creation, you know. Although she was often wiped out personally by these

problems. The other interesting thing to me was that Holiday was one of the very few major black singers who was not influenced directly by the church, and that allowed her to give voice to an urban song and heartache that was a combination of at least three things: blues, and also the tradition of the cabaret singer, and the eloquence of jazz, particularly the jazz horn men. And she was fascinating for that. In other words, we were talking about a completely different voice . . . from Dinah Washington and from so many of the black singers who were influenced directly by the church, sang out in church, came out of the church. And so we're talking about soul. She had soul. But it was a different kind of soul. It allowed her, because she wasn't overwhelmed by the simplicity of acceptance of faith inherent in the church, it allowed her, perhaps even forced her, to think in a most savvy and cunning way about these sentimental lyrics that she sang. So Holiday also transcended the sort of tinpan alley Broadway song she sang with something that's sea-soned and sassy and evil and lyrical quite all her own. So long before I ever thought about all that, you know, there she was in my mind. So it's wonderful to have some of this stuff in your background long before you start to write or paint, to draw on. But again, the writer has to get that kind of detachment to think in an analytical way about his or her own sources . . . even as you are nourished by them in a sort of natural way.

**Warren:** Is that an ongoing process of detachment?
**Forrest:** Yes, and you have to have both . . . I'm often knocked down by fig-ures like Holiday. And then Charlie Parker . . . reading certain writers. I have to sort of come back up again . . . But then there's always the other side that says, "Well, wait a minute now. I'd better try to think a minute about this."

**Warren:** Take that into a reflection of literature, say, at the present moment. Who are the writers who . . . ?
**Forrest:** Knock me down? Probably the last would have been Marquez, I guess.

**Warren:** *One Hundred Years of Solitude*?
**Forrest:** *Autumn of the Patriarch*, too. There are writers out there, but after a while, you know, you know, you get so cold and you're sort of reading a writer and asking, "Well, let me see what he's doing technically." well, another writer who fascinates me is Walcott. But usually, I'm reading something I've

read a long time ago, over and over again, you know, to find some of these resources, any energizing resources in his or her work.

**Warren:** Well, thanks a lot. I enjoyed this very much.
**Forrest:** Well thank *you*.

**Warren:** We'll have to do it again.

# The Mythos of Gumbo: Leon Forrest Talks about *Divine Days*

Madhu Dubey / 1994

From *Callaloo* 19:3 (1996) 588–602. © by Charles H. Rowell. Reprinted with permission of The Johns Hopkins University Press.

**Madhu Dubey:** Let's begin with the most immediately striking aspect of *Divine Days*—its length. Did you consciously set out to write a novel of epic scope, or did the novel expand as you were in the process of writing it?
**Leon Forrest:** Well, I certainly set out to write a novel of epic scope, but I didn't know it would have to be this long. Actually the comedy and humor kept me going, in terms of just interest, and I thought that since I was interested in it, maybe a readership would be interested in it as well.

**Dubey:** Was there an initial conception or seed in your mind from which the novel took shape?
**Forrest:** Well, sure there was. One was that it would be over a seven-day period. I had been reading and rereading in recent time *Ulysses*, with the great power that book has over one day, so I thought that might be intriguing to try over seven days. Also the character of Sugar Groove was one that fascinated me throughout the course of the novel. And I would say Ford. And then I was quite fascinated later in the novel by the possibilities of the character Imani. It seems to me many major novels center on at least three major characters, so I was driven along by fascination with each of these characters, but each in a different way.

**Dubey:** Did the novel change as you were writing it—your idea of what you wanted to achieve in it?
**Forrest:** No, it seemed to expand a lot. One of my concerns was to try to write a novel that would capture the complexity of African American character, so that I wanted to see characters in sustained series of development.

Well, you need a long novel to do that. But that's one of my criticisms of much of just modern fiction anyway, that you rarely get characters who are developed in depth.

**Dubey:** Did you write the novel in a linear fashion, beginning with what is now the beginning of the novel, and going straight through until the end?
**Forrest:** Oh no. One of the first scenes that I wrote would have been the one in the barbershop, when they're telling this long tall tale about Sugar Groove.

**Dubey:** Throughout the novel, the narrator, Joubert Jones, who is himself an aspiring writer, remarks on the temptation of imposing a simplistic order on the chaos of experience. And clearly the structure of *Divine Days* resists that kind of temptation. Is it accurate to say that the structure of the novel is modeled on a jazz method of composition—a method which allows you to give shape to chaos without imposing a kind of reductive order on it?
**Forrest:** It is. Chaos is a great driving force in all life. It's a driving force in just the basic things of life, because when we get up in the morning we're faced with chaos . . . I guess though that for me the first connection with jazz is that I will take just a fragment of a story, or a fragment of a character, or a confrontation, and then build on it, build on it, riff on it like a jazz musician or a solo performer. So in fact a lot of scenes just start off with me working on a little riff, and then that develops into a scene. As far as the larger thing goes, I always try to orchestrate a scene so that it starts off in one way, gets involved with some other things, and then comes back to that—a little fugue-like method. But I'm always trying to both orchestrate a scene and orchestrate the novel really, as well as do those individual solos. And they're all through there—remember the long one with Beefeater, for instance, and the one we were talking about in the barbershop. And there are many others.

**Dubey:** In fact, I think at one place in the novel you refer to a rambling method of storytelling as akin to riffing in a jazz piece.
**Forrest:** Yes, yes.

**Dubey:** You use the phrase "mythos of gumbo" in the novel, and taking it completely out of context, I read this phrase as a really eloquent description of what you achieve in the novel—the way that you manage this complex mix of languages and cultures without reaching for a kind of false or easy coherence.

**Forrest:** Well, thank you. You see, for me writing is one place where I can get leverage over all this chaos that appears so livid and volatile in my imagination, and I can't get it any other place. I can't get it in conversation . . . So also a way of dealing with my own loneliness, I guess, is to be able to find a place where I can bring all of this together, and create a certain mad world out of it.

**Dubey:** It was clear to me from reading the novel that your understanding of African-American culture is strongly opposed to any kind of purist or singular conception of cultural identity, or even a bifocal conception. I'm thinking here of the various references in the novel to the Du Boisian notion of double-consciousness as confining, or even your satire on Fulton Armstead's double A. Could you elaborate on what precisely you find so confining about these?

**Forrest:** I resist anything in this culture that has to do with purity. That's so anti-American in the first place. And yet at the same time it's crucible on which so much of race relations and white supremacy is based—the idea of purity. But there certainly aren't any pure Americans culturally, not at this time, that's one thing for sure. And obviously the heritage, the background of blacks is very complex, not just on color lines but lines of culture. Think about the blacks that are most admired—whether it be Ellington, or Lightnin Hopkins, or Mahalia, or Leontyne Price—these are people who are consequences of so many different cultural forms that influenced them, and out of that they fashioned something new. Armstrong maybe is the best example.

**Dubey:** Do you find that taking this kind of position is unpopular these days?

**Forrest:** It's not so much a taking of a position. Rather, it's almost like a religious faith to me. But it's a faith that I've come to evolve into or have been converted into through my own experience in life.

**Dubey:** What are some of the experiences that led you to believe this so strongly?

**Forrest:** Well, a good background in African American music of all kinds, and certainly literature, a sense of the complexity of democracy, and the way in which other groups impact upon us. Many of the nationalists don't want to deal with that. And the best proof always is, of course—let a true African come into the room and you can see how American blacks are.

**Dubey:** Why do you insist on using the term "Negro-American" in the novel? What does the term signify to you that "black American" or "African American" doesn't?
**Forrest:** I don't look at it as a bad word. I don't have a problem with any of those terms, although many of the characters in my novel would really have been—don't forget the novel is set in 1966—more what we would call traditional Negroes in the sense of being race men, race women. So that's part of it. But I don't have any problems with the terms "black" or . . .

**Dubey:** What about your satirical play on the double A, for African American?
**Forrest:** Oh yeah. Well again, there's the setting, and there's a lot of satire in there. Actually, of course, Fulton is a very nice guy. He's like many people who are rather limited or bigoted on some things, but they can be very warm with certain groups within their tribe or tradition, even as they're exclusive to outsiders. So he represents some of that, but meanwhile if you remember in the novel he's made a fool of by many of the Africans who see how hung up he is.

**Dubey:** I'm going to take another phrase from your novel out of context—"swirl of identities"—which perfectly captures the way in which identify in *Divine Days* is never unified or unitary, but is always a melange of other people's voices and languages. And throughout the novel, characters are obsessed and even possessed by other people's voices which force them to revise and expand their own sense of their identities.
**Forrest:** That's certainly true with Joubert. Of course that's so much a part of the vision of the novel—the transformation of the self constantly, impact of other cultures, other individuals, and so on, on the individual. In that sense, the characters are hopefully a little bit like Proteus in *The Odyssey*. Certainly Sugar Groove is that way.

**Dubey:** And Ford, and so many others.
**Forrest:** The people who aren't are the ones who get in trouble, like Imani. I think that that's such a wonderful feature of black American life, this capacity

for reinvention, of taking whatever it is and making something new out of it, constantly, You've got to do that if you're a jazz musician. You've got to do that if you're a preacher. You've got to do that if you're a gospel singer—make it new each night, make it different. And that in turn carries over to the whole quest for identity—to try to find out new ways of engaging oneself and transforming oneself and one's identity, given American society.

**Dubey:** In the novel, you treat so many different facets of African American culture with a kind of generous irony that celebrates at the same time as it debunks. And I found that the only group that you subject to merciless satire are the nationalists. I'm especially thinking of the character of Sambi! Are you unambivalently critical of black nationalist ideologies, or do you see any redeeming or necessary features in them?

**Forrest:** Well, I think there are a lot of redeeming qualities that maybe even Joubert doesn't see about someone like Fulton, even though he's made a fool of sometimes. He's very generous; he certainly is in the tradition of race men, trying to take care of the tribe. But he's lost the cutting edge which would let him see how people will take advantage of him. There's a wonderful generous spirit about him that I do admire in certain features of nationalism, the spirit of taking care of your own. But the point is that in this country there are so many other ways in which taking care of your own can be impacted upon by the outer culture that he's cut himself off from completely. I mean, he has a hell of a time that night when some whites take Felton home. He can't deal with that, you know. So I see him and Sambi! as quite different. Sambi! is more of a sinister and demonic trickster, and in that sense he's connected a little bit with Ford.

**Dubey:** Yes. In Your interview with Ken Warren, you said that you don't believe that the Black Aesthetic of the 1960s generated any significant artistic developments.

**Forrest:** Certainly not in the novel.

**Dubey:** I just wanted to push you a little further on this. Do you think the cultural nationalists' emphasis on recovering black oral forms catalyzed the way in which so much subsequent black fiction experiments with oral forms?

Or would you trace that back earlier, to, say, Ralph Ellison, or even the Harlem Renaissance?

**Forrest:** That's right. And Sterling Brown, and so on. I'm not a scholar of this, but I suppose that there was some residue that came off that was useful to many of the writers who emerged. I didn't need it, but maybe some of the younger people did. That may well be true. But ultimately the people who are successful who came out of that, let's say, like Alice Walker and later Toni, and many others—they've vaulted over so much of the narrows of the Black Aesthetic. The Black Aesthetic also on some levels was very chauvinistic, so many of the women who emerged in the 1970s had to vault over it for those reasons as well. But I didn't particularly need it, and it was never complicated enough for me. Again, my point initially was that there were many poets who came out of there, of dubious quality, or various qualities. Many of them haven't survived. But in terms of the novel, hardly any novelists that I can think of.

**Dubey:** Did it even have a negative impact on your work during that period?

**Forrest:** Well, it had a negative impact in the sense that I felt that I wasn't going to be published by any of this crowd, which was true. They weren't interested in what I was saying. But I find that negative forces are oftentimes quite useful, quite useful. There's a little saying my mother used to have. It wasn't very profound, but she used to say, "Every knock is a boost." No, if anything, it sort of toughened my resolve. Because it wasn't question of right or wrong, but it was rather that I knew there was a whole lot about black life out here that they had no sense of.

**Dubey:** Do you feel that the cultural climate, especially in the universities, has changed substantially since the 1960s and 1970s?

**Forrest:** I don't know if it's improved for the better in some ways. It's certainly much more open to black writers and African American culture and so on. But there's still a tendency to find a certain catalogue of heroines and heroes, and this means that other people who are very good and who don't tend to fall into a certain line are excluded or are undervalued. Or there's a tendency now, since so many black writers have emerged—not really a lot but seemingly a lot—to say, Oh, you're in so-and-so's school. You're in the Ellison school. Or you're in the Morrison school. Or you're in the . . . may be Baraka School, if there's one. And meanwhile writers underneath a school or spell are very different. They'd say that, let's say, about Gayl Jones under Morrison, but her work is very different. My works is, I would hope, very different from Ellison's, though it's certainly benefited greatly by his impact.

**Dubey:** In a recent interview-essay on Ralph Ellison in *The New Yorker* David Remnick claims that Ellison's three books, the novel and the two collections of essays, "are the texts for a loose coalition of black American intellectuals who represent an integrationist vision of the country's history and culture," and among these intellectuals, Remnick names you, along with Wideman and Charles Johnson. I have two questions about this. First, do you find it accurate to say that Ellison's works generated a group of black authors who represent an integrationist vision? And, secondly, if you were to place yourself in a loose coalition of authors, which ones would you select? Would it be Ellison and Wideman and Johnson, or would you place yourself in an entirely different set?

**Forrest:** No, I'd add some writers to that I'd be very honored to be in that group; that's a very fine group of writers. Ultimately, though, what you would do would be to take certain books from each of those writers, rather than to say all of Gaines's work, or all of Forrest's. You might say, "Well, now *this* is of a certain level." And that's the bad thing about ever saying, "I like the work of this writer," because it means you like all of Hardy, or all of this one or that one, which you obviously do not necessarily do. Even Faulkner, my goodness, he's so uneven, you know. The other thing is that the statement is alright for a magazine article because it's got to constantly distill things. But I never felt any sort of constitution that was set forth by Ellison that I had to follow at all. I benefited greatly by his experience and learned a great many things from him, but my work is very different in other ways. I'm much more interested in problems of families, religion—these two issues alone are issues that Ellison doesn't deal with a lot, at least in the published work. So even as I salute so much of what he's done and his example, I also, if I'm worth anything, want to say, "Yes, but this is my church over here, and this is his church, and then this is another person's church." And the singing is different, the preaching is different, even though we're all Baptists, let's say.

**Dubey:** What are some of the ways that Ellison's writing has influenced not just your writing but also the last few generations of black writers?

**Forrest:** Again, I would say this whole idea of transformation of oral eloquence into literary eloquence. That's been an impact that he's had on a great many writers in various ways. It's not so much to say that he was the only writer who was doing that, but he seemed to be the one who was most successful in doing that, in fiction. Baldwin was doing that in the essay form . . .

**Dubey:** And there was Zora Neale Hurston . . .

**Forrest:** Well, the problem would have been that a lot of people of my generation probably wouldn't have read Hurston the way we would have read Ellison in college.

**Dubey:** Simply because her books weren't available?

**Forrest:** That's right. Another thing is, it really does help a writer if someone else's work is celebrated, so that you say, "Oh yes, this is someone who must be taken seriously, and here's all this body of criticism behind it." So you really want to tip your hat to, let's say, Alice Walker, who discovered Hurston on her own and saw the strengths there.

**Dubey:** A lot of the recent criticism on African American fiction focuses on the distinctive ways in which this fiction draws on oral forms. In *Divine Days*, for example, you evoke a wide variety of these forms, including blues, jazz, storytelling, sermons, and so on. Yet clearly you're not a musician or a preacher or a storyteller, but you're a novelist. Often this crucial distinction between an oral artist and a novelist tends to get blurred in the criticism. In what ways do you think that your work as a novelist both overlaps with and differs from an oral performance?

**Forrest:** Well, ultimately, I want to be judged as a novelist and not an oral artist. And in that sense I would diverge somewhat at least from Morrison's public statements about that. Ultimately I want to weigh on the eloquence of the written heritage that has the complexity of scripture to it. I'm much more influenced by other writers in that sense, but at the same time I want to keep alive that grain, that personality, that ethos that is so African American. The jazz musicians are very helpful for that because I can hear all kinds of cries and groans and screeches of various kinds in the solo of an alto saxophonist, let us say, that I can identify with certain street cries and so on. But at the same time there's a certain lyricism there that is the lyricism of a surging songster that can only be done through the refinement of art by the musician. And just as that street cry that it may be based on is a long way from the eloquence of what you'd hear in, let's say, Ellington's band, the imagination allows us to connect both.

**Dubey:** You're clearly not interested in merely reproducing or transcribing oral forms. Could you say something about the process of refinement, as you call it, by which you transform oral forms into fiction?
**Forrest:** Well, I get it through tradition, but I also get it through just the hard work or rewriting over and over again.

**Dubey:** Do you read aloud to yourself sometimes?
**Forrest:** Yes, I do. Although ultimately I've got to mistrust as well as trust the ear because reading, as we know, is done in silence. And even as we encourage our students to read aloud, ultimately reading is done in solitude, just as writing is done in solitude. And you are thinking and meditating and reflecting as you're reading. So even if in class we have someone read aloud, we've got to stop that after a while because you get hypnotized by the prose of this writer or that writer and then you say, well, now let's go back and investigate what he or she is doing. It is a reflective art in that sense, but it comes through rewriting endlessly, putting it away and coming back to it, and cutting out what might well be the fat of it or also perhaps certain things that are too pedestrian in the writing. And I think also what's important is training your ear at an early age on a variety of rhetorical sounds—being open to that, being a good listener. Then I think too being willing to allow characters to speak with many voices. People speak with many voices, and those many voices suggest to me a layered consciousness.

**Dubey:** You referred a moment ago to Toni Morrison's statement about what she calls the tribal artist or the village artist. In one of her essays, "Rootedness: The Ancestor as Foundation," she writes that the novelist is needed urgently now in the African American community, to fill the place or to serve the same kinds of functions as were served by the tribal artist in the past. Is it even possible for the contemporary novelist to replace the oral performer? Aren't the audiences for these two kinds of artists vastly different?
**Forrest:** I think so. What she wants to do, and it's understandable, is to get some kind of connection really, to open up things for the writer. And she can do this, because Morrison can have a house full of people who will listen to

her in the way a tribal artist was listened to at one time, or a griot. That's a great power that she has and it's hard to think of any other American writer, black or white, who has that kind of power with an audience. And this is an old thing. You remember in the 1960s maybe and a little later too, when the poets would go around to cabarets and so on and read their poetry aloud, to try to bridge the gap between these worlds. It's all quite commendable, but for me anyway it's a different tradition. They have connections, and the connection is the imagination. As you were saying, people were listening the other night to what I was reading and found music in it . . . But it would be only in thinking about it in a mood that's quite reflective that they'd say, "I think this is what it's about." What they were doing was hearing echoes of the tradition, but they weren't necessarily seeing where it was taking them imaginatively. I guess also you'd have to say that event thought Toni says these things, her work is fascinating through the imagination, through fantasy.

**Dubey:** Also, the kind of audience that reads Toni Morrison's work or your work is very different from the kind of audience that she has in mind or anyone has in mind when they speak of tribal art.
**Forrest:** That's right. And there is a danger, of course. No matter whatever else we say, we're not finally preachers, really.

**Dubey:** Do you have an ideal audience in mind when you write?
**Forrest:** I don't. I just think of probably people who would want to approach literature the way I like to approach it, as an art of infinite resonance, that you can go back to again and again, and get nourishment and intellectual stimulation and fun, and all the things you need to live.

**Dubey:** So you don't write for any particular group, let's say, for example, black readers or literary critics?
**Forrest:** No, no, no! Male, female, black, white . . . Maybe if I had the good sense to do that, I would sell more.

**Dubey:** While reading *Divine Days*, I was constantly struck by the very non-purist ways in which oral and folk forms appear in the novel. Throughout, oral and literary influences, high culture and popular culture, all interact in often really startling ways. For example, Cinderella, a girl from the West-side projects, writes Shakespearean sonnets, and Joubert quotes Joyce to

Williemain the barber. Is there a utopian impulse behind your creation of these fluent dialogues between different sections of the black community? Does it project a way of overcoming potentially divisive class and educational differences within the community?

**Forrest:** Well, no, it's really there. Don't forget, with Cinderella, that's one of the last things we find out about her and there are a lot of other things that are more dominant about her—being lost, a little waif, and so on. And really, if you think about it, in a city like Chicago, for years you had the influence of Gwendolyn Brooks with this contest, and Brooks herself, of course. Many of these poems of hers were based on a kind of pure form and it's not unusual that a teacher would help a child who is wayward and lost in every other way. I was trying to write against this idea of a child who's totally a victim, although she's certainly a victim in many ways. And of course for a long time she can hardly talk and then when she gets in the cab, she just can't stop. So she herself is full of contradictions, and obviously I'm writing this against images like Bigger or maybe even Pecola. Not to say they're wrong at all, because we get more and more the sense that Wright was really on to something about Bigger. But there are some other sides to characters who come from this situation that are rarely conveyed to us in terms of literature.

**Dubey:** Another striking example of what one can call a gumbo method of mixing cultural forms in the novel is the character of Sugar Groove, whose cultural ancestry includes Oedipus, Icarus, the black folk figures of the trickster and the badman, and even the legendary flying African. Early on in the novel, each time I came across Sugar Groove's character, it recalled Luzana Cholly from Albert Murray's *Train Whistle Guitar*. But later I found that despite all the parallels, there are clear differences, because Luzana Cholly is a pure folk type while Sugar Groove's character stretches the bounds of folk heroism—for example, he's college educated, and he's highly literate. Could you talk a little about the ways in which you reinvent the folk figure of the badman, with specific deference to Sugar Groove?

**Forrest:** I'm glad you mentioned Luzana Cholly. I hadn't thought about it in a while, but I certainly at one time was teaching that book regularly and found him a fascinating character. That's the first time anyone has mentioned that. Again, you're writing against figures you admire in literature and in life, so I didn't want to repeat that figure, and I wanted to create someone who had this range of complexity. Certainly, there are a lot of things about Sugar

Groove that are symbolic of a certain generation of African American hustler, and drifter, and a man who collected everything along the way. And it turns out he's also quite a generous an and apparently goes through this spiritual turning late in his life. I would always see people somewhat like this who would go through some late spiritual transformation or had a certain kind of inwardness. But because on the surface there was such a bravado about their lives—women, drink, and gambling—people would miss this interior loneliness, or this interior cry of the soul. So I wanted to explore that. Like Sugar Groove, these were people who would disappear for a long time and come back with their travels and what they had done. That disappearing and coming back was part of the legendary quality of these figures. But these are personality attributes within the community that are just waiting out there for some artist to come and seize and give a shape to. You're not sure about it, but there are some things you've seen at times—they may be good, they may be bad, they may be a mix of both—but they need to be addressed. I felt that certainly with the history of itinerant jazz musicians, blues singers, drifters, people who wandered around the city and so on—Sugar Groove was in that traditions as well as having some formal education.

**Dubey:** Another sense in which Sugar Groove's character seems to revise the type of the badman is in his relationships with women. In so much of the fiction of Toni Morrison and Alice Walker, you get a critique of the badman because of his irresponsibility and his often damaging effects on women. As far as Sugar Groove is concerned, did you consciously set out to redeem that aspect of the outlaw or badman figure?
**Forrest:** Well, I wanted to make it a little bit more complicated because, don't forget, he does stop seeing his daughter, event though he sends money regularly, and I think that's something to be criticized about him, even though he's still in search for her.

**Dubey:** Yet at the same time he acts in a very responsible way toward Imani.
**Forrest:** Yes, She comes on and . . .

**Dubey:** Very uncharacteristic of that type of . . .
**Forrest:** Here again I don't like the word "type" perhaps when I come to my main characters. I might have some types who are very minor. But certainly there's no type with him though you do see some traditions that he comes

out of. And then you remembers there's this whole scene when Sweetie tells him, "don't use this as an excuse for not seeing your daughter." She tells him off, you know.

**Dubey:** It's not just in relation to women but even in his relationship with Joubert that Sugar Groove emerges as a deeply responsible and even a spiritually redemptive figure. In your interview with Ken Warren, you said that "the trickster is the one who is not an agent of healing." I wondered about that, because isn't Sugar Groove a trickster who's also a healer? I'm thinking particularly of the episode with Tilly Taylor, when he disguises himself as a gypsy fortune-teller in order to perform his good works.
**Forrest:** See, that's why I wouldn't say that he was a badman so much, but more of a kind of hipster, hipster-trickster as angel. I don't see him in the tradition of the badman. I see him more as a drifter who's searching for his identity but continues to search. That goes back to your earlier question, the idea that the search is constant. And never to think that if I settle upon this, this, and this, that'll do it. In fact, you remember he breaks with the Civil Rights movement because that wouldn't deal enough with the violence in him. So he's ultimately back to that relationship to some spiritual force within human nature.

**Dubey:** Do you see any kind of relationship between the trickster as healer and the trickster as demon? Both sugar Groove and Ford are trickster figures.
**Forrest:** Of course, Ford is a trickster as demon, diabolical and so on. Here we might think about when Wilkerson talks about the difference between some of the African and African American tricksters. And Sugar Groove veers on this idea of using his devices, his tricks, for healing, bringing people together. But don't forget, he does this in a way that is selfish, in the sense that he can hardly remember these people's names, you know, and he gives them names. The novel is filled with all sorts of tricksters, and one of the problems with Imani is that she doesn't have enough of that in her personality, and so she's constantly being set up by people. And to some degree—this gets us back to Ford—it's necessary to have some of that in the base of human personality, and yet not to go to the point of Ford, who is so base and so treacherous, and yet comic, I hope, in a certain way, too. So sugar Groove would represent in many ways, not all ways, the trickster as healer. He's always trying to bring things together, bring people together, even though

some tricks were often played by him in the South, you remember, with his father and so on. So he represents a certain magical force, a trying to bring order out of chaos. Ford is on the other end of the spectrum, someone who delights in chaos. There may be a connection here between Ford and Rinehart in *Invisible Man*, who feeds on chaos. And of course chaos destroys the so-attractive Tod Clifton . . . I thought it was important too that the last part of sugar Groove's life in the novel revealed that he's really trying to come together with his spiritual force.

**Dubey:** Yes, I kept thinking of the two characters together—Sugar Groove and Ford—because of the ambiguity of the title itself. On the one hand Joubert has written a play called *Divine Days* about Ford. Yet at the start of the novel, he says he'd like to write a play about the "divine days" of Sugar Groove. That double reference kept making me think of the ways in which the two characters are so close to and yet distinct from each other.
**Forrest:** Oh, sure. And there's a certain energy that Ford has that may be the energy that drives the world, before we refine it to some levels, like a Sugar Groove; and even there, Sugar Groove himself is a man who is always in search of his identity, and seemingly by the time he was seventy he had finally embraced it.

**Dubey:** Would you agree that Joubert's greatest artistic rival in the novel is Ford, who is described as the ultimate playwright?
**Forrest:** That's true, but he's also Sugar Groove's greatest rival for the attention, I would think, of the reader.

**Dubey:** As a portrait of the artist as a young man, *Divine Days* presents a model of the relationship between the artist and tradition which recalls Ellison's famous remarks on the relation between each individual jazz musician and the prior tradition. Could you say something about that?
**Forrest:** There are two scenes that we could focus on in which you have this "antagonistic cooperation"—this is Ellison's term and he sort of did an improvisation of Eliot, I guess. One is the scene between Joubert and Reverend Roper. In this scene, Reverend Roper attempts to make something of a conversion of Joubert, but he feels that, to bring him to the other side, he must meet him on the grounds of the secular. And then they go back and forth like two jazz musicians trying to outblow each other or duel

each other. Ultimately it would appear that this is what Ellison was talking about—there's a lot of fun between the two men as they try to outdo each other in storytelling and these storytelling riffs are really like aspects of jazz. And the other scene that comes to mind is in the barbershop between Williemain and Joubert in which they're arguing over, debating, in some cases supplanting knowledge that the other has, in some cases agreeing, and that is connected to what happens in oral tradition between a speaker and a congregation. And ultimately the reader will want to decide how these two set pieces, between Roper and Joubert, and between Joubert and Williemain, are similar and yet different. Those are two different jazz sets, you see.

**Dubey:** Could your own relationship with literary figures whom you've admired also be described as an "antagonistic cooperation"?
**Forrest:** Consciously and unconsciously, yes. And that would certainly be true, as you called to mind—I'd even forgotten about this—with the whole character of Luzana Cholly of Murray's. It probably did influence my writing of Sugar Groove. And that has to do with the fact that many writers identify a certain kind of figure within the culture, and then each spends a lifetime giving particular shape to him or her.

**Dubey:** One African American novelist that I don't hear you talk much about is Richard Wright, and considering that you both write about Chicago, what is it about his work that you find doesn't engage you as, say, Ellison's or Murray's does?
**Forrest:** I'm engaged by Wright in teaching him but less engaged by him in terms of influence. The other thing is, and I was talking to you a little bit about this with Hemingway, that a lot of times a writer can free you to do certain things. A lot of things Wright dealt with in Chicago with Bigger have freed me to go on and do something completely different, and something I'm more familiar with about Chicago.

**Dubey:** Would you elaborate on that?
**Forrest:** Well, I wouldn't want to create another Bigger, even though I admired what he did with Bigger. And seemingly, given all the lost young males in the slums and so on, he was really on to something about the importance of Bigger. But I wouldn't want to do that. I would want to get

involved with characters who are much more complicated. Wright could never have created a character like Aunt Eloise, for instance. Wright rarely creates any really memorable dimensional women. And I'm extremely drawn to the complexity of female characters in all of my novels, and in my private life. And then Wright's own background, from Mississippi, was so hard, and my life has been very different. But there are certain things that he does—for instance, "Fire and Cloud" is just an amazing story, and I go back to that. But I guess since he was dealing with certain harsh realities of black life, in the South and in the North, it allowed me then to think about how I can get in-depth characterization. I think this is just a normal thing that a writer does—whether you admire a writer a lot or are influenced by him or not, you want to make sure you're cutting your own little path, your own little postage stamp.

**Dubey:** Talking about complex female characters: in conversation the other day, you mentioned that you weren't completely happy with the way you had treated the character of Imani in *Divine Days*. What was it that you wanted to do with her character, but felt that you didn't?

**Forrest:** There are things I would have liked to have gone into about her, and I may well do that in the next novel. But that's a problem of writing a novel—maybe that's one reason why people work on a book for so long—because there are constantly new questions asked. I feel pretty complete about the other characters, but there is a heartbreak and a humanity that I wanted to get at with her, and I don't know that I've been able to get at all the depths of her personality.

**Dubey:** Is there anything else that you feel you didn't manage to do in *Divine Days* as you wished to?

**Forrest:** There probably will be things as I read it over again over a period of time. A friend of mine I won't name had said that he thought—I'm giving a part of it away already—that I might have muted the section on Beefeater, that it was too long. He was comparing it with other sections that he found had such power but that seemed to be too diffuse, I guess.

**Dubey:** So you don't feel that this novel is completed or over with? Do you still think of going back and editing?

**Forrest:** Oh no, I won't touch it now. You have to draw the line eventually and say, "This is it." I certainly wouldn't edit anything. Even though I respect this person's criticism, I'm too bull-headed to ever go back and change anything. Then also I want to move on to something else. But Imani may well be one of the characters who may grow within me. That's the other thing, you never know who may grow within you. I'd like to do some more things with Sugar Groove, but as of this moment I don't know what.

**Dubey:** The new novel you're working on, is it haunted by *Divine Days*?
**Forrest:** Well, yes, it is, because *Divine Days* is such a mighty work, mighty in terms of my own imagination. So I've got at least three problems. One, to outwrite it, to write a better novel—not a longer one, but a better one. Also to find something in my cranium where it's not dominating.

**Dubey:** Is it dominating your writing these days?
**Forrest:** Yes, it's still a very dominating force, as you might imagine, with 1829 pages and seven years in the writing. I don't know how much I've recouped. . . . It's almost like being in love with someone and then you break off with them. You've been going with them or married to them seven years. That's good time, seven years—the seven-year itch. And then you leave and break away from them, but you can't ever get that man or that woman out of your mind.

**Dubey:** Do you want to say something about the new novel that you're working on, or is it too early?
**Forrest:** No, it's alright. I don't have any problems with that at all. It'll be about six or seven novellas, and they all make up a novel. And it won't be in the first person; it'll be omniscient. Some of it picks up material from *Divine Days*, and then other stuff is completely new. I have a few tricksters in there though.

**Dubey:** Is this going to be another seven years?
**Forrest:** I don't know. I hope not. I don't think so. With my health, I don't even know if I have seven years. No, it won't be as long. It'll probably be, say, seven or eight-hundred manuscript pages. Six or seven novellas. I've already written two of them. And there are some characters from my other novels that'll be in there. I don't know if you remember a woman by the name of Lucasta Jones. She's in there, she has a large role in there, and I'm finding I'm more and more engaged by her character. Joubert is in there, Aunt Elosie, and there are some completely new characters, one or two poets, and so on.

# Leon Forrest at the University of Kentucky: On *There Is a Tree More Ancient than Eden*

John G. Cawelti / 1994

From *Leon Forrest: Introductions and Interpretations* by John G. Cawelti (Madison, WI: University of Wisconsin Press, 1997). © 1997 by John G. Cawelti. Reprinted by permission.

**John Cawelti:** This is a session with Leon Forrest where we'll go around the table with every person having a chance to ask a question.

**Student:** (Asks about Forrest's relationship to the Harlem Renaissance and whether he had met Louis Armstrong.)
**Forrest:** No, I didn't know Armstrong, but listened to him all the time. My great uncle went to school with him in New Orleans and knew him a bit. I certainly am in the tradition of the experimental African American novelists. I guess the thing I would resist, of course, would be that the only writers who influenced me were African American. My influences are all across the board like Ellison. I'm interested in breakthroughs in writing and the novel form, and even poetry wherever they happen. I am indebted to all of these writers. Then out of my reading and my experiences, I try to reshape something that has my own stamp to it and that is how style evolves.

**Student:** I have a question dealing with the "Lives" section of *There Is a Tree More Ancient than Eden*. It seems to bear a strong resemblance to the "Appendix" to Faulkner's *The Sound and the Fury*.
**Forrest:** It certainly does. When I studied *The Sound and the Fury* for the first time at the University of Chicago, the "Appendix" was at the beginning of the book. Now they have it at the end. It was helpful having it at the beginning. I had actually written all of *There Is a Tree*, the 1973 version, and my editor, Toni Morrison said that in order to sell this to her fellow editors, the book needed some kind of introduction. She was fascinated by the material, but

without some understanding of the characters which glue the text together it
was too difficult to understand. Actually, the novel as it was originally written
began with Chapter 2. I went back and wrote "Lives" and I did get the idea
from Faulkner. No doubt about that. I wrote all of that in about two months,
I was so hot to have a contract.

But I also like the idea of the competition. I knew that Faulkner wrote the
"Appendix" about 15 years after the novel. It is wonderful material. Here was
a chance to "box" the old man. No matter how much the young writer
admires the older one, if he is worth anything he wants to beat him. That's
probably a male perspective.

**Student:** Was it a conscious decision to place it at the beginning?
**Forrest:** Oh, sure. I had to have something to help the reader get into the
book. Faulkner offered a way and I was going to see if I could use that and
then beat him at his game. That may be egotistical, but that's the way it was.
The first section of the book that was actually published was in a little magazine called *Blackbird*. That was actually Chapter 3, which starts on page 46. It
was originally called "That's your little red wagon." The phrase is kind of a
put-down in African American culture. It is a wild chapter in a book that is
not known for modesty.

The reason that I went to Random House with the manuscript was this:
One of the editors of the Muslim paper *Muhammad Speaks*, where I worked at
the time, had a contact with Holt, Rinehart who had published Toni Morrison's
novel *The Bluest Eye* in 1970. I sent the manuscript to them and the editor liked
it a lot, but said "I can't make sense of it." He said, "You might send it to Toni
Morrison, who is an editor at Random House and recently promoted. She
might be interested." So, I called there and at that time, you could get right
through to her. She was sitting at her desk. So I described the manuscript. She
said, "That sounds interesting. Send it to me." I did. She called me back the
next week. I went up to New York to review a play by Melvin van Peebles for
*Muhammad Speaks*. Morrison and I met and I gave her the section that was
published in *Blackbird* Magazine. That was helpful to her in arguing with the
other editors to get it published. You know how that works in a company. All of
you are editors. If you have a manuscript you are interested in, you've got to
convince the other people around the table. It is sort of a collective thing.

Morrison was a very good editor on several levels. She was an excellent
line editor. She, too, is very much caught up in language. We had a tough

fight to get my works through at Random House. She had to do some boxing there. I like to think that eventually I would have been published, but at the time I could not have done it without Morrison's help. She was indispensable. You must have a literary agent, today.

**Student:** You can't just make a phone call?

**Forrest:** No, nothing as simple at that. As I mentioned, I wrote the "Lives" section after this. One of the things I was trying to do was to reconsider what I had already written. "Lives" ends with a section on Abraham Lincoln. I don't know which section is the heart of the book and I really don't even like to use that term, but the Lincoln section is pretty important in that it reflects the savagery of America. It's pulling up a leader and then destroying him. It's the way we use up things. African American music has been used in this way, becoming tainted and destroyed by being commercialized, then corrupted.

**Student:** Is this linked in with the "Transformations" section which you added later?

**Forrest:** The tension between destruction and resurrection, between death and rebirth, is central to *There Is a Tree* and this idea was instrumental in my decision to add the last two sections when the novel was republished. This section includes Sweetie Reed's letter, which is about the way the effigy of Johnson is destroyed, and the sermon on Martin Luther King, which is also about leadership and its destruction. The "Lives" section ends with Lincoln and now the novel itself ends with King, great leaders of the 19th and 20th century. The tension between the destruction and resurrection of leaders is also summed up at the end of the "Vision" section. Then there is an attempt to gather up what is left over in this remnant.

The "Lives" section is quite stark with many destroyed lives, Jamestown Fishbond, M. C. Browne, Lincoln, even the little section about Stale-Bread Winters who has such great potential and is driven to destroy himself. Many people, like Breedlove, develop great strength and survive. Louis Armstrong is an example. These people survive through the strength of several resources in black culture. These are the remnants of hope within the "Lives" section, as exemplified in Hattie Breedlove Wordlaw, Louis Armstrong, Frederick Douglass, Harriet Tubman, Jericho Witherspoon and Taylor "Warm Gravy" James, the jazz musician. They represent sources of strength in African

American life. Music, certain powerful historical figures of affirmation, and the tradition of religious faith.

**Cawelti:** I think you said that *There Is a Tree* was originally titled "Wakefulness." How did you happen to decide on using a different title?
**Forrest:** That was Morrison's idea, and it was an excellent one, too. It was Morrison who gave me, ultimately, a title for the book. We had gone round and round on it. I sent her 40 titles one weekend. I wasn't sure of what it should be called.

**Cawelti:** What were some of your early ideas for a title?
**Forrest:** They were outlandish. I can do a pretty good title as a newspaper man and was nifty at headlines for other peoples' stories, but the title of my book was different. I suggested "Deep Rivers of the Soul." At one point we were calling it "Of Eden and Thebes." Eventually Morrison came up with the idea of *There Is a Tree More Ancient than Eden.* I liked it very much. It seemed close to a Negro spiritual. For her, it may also have implied some African themes. Morrison also had the idea of using a different type face for the "Vision" section. It was helpful, I thought. You know she was easy to work with. The copy editor and even the person who sets the type are important in making a book.

**Student:** I wanted to ask about the section where Jamestown and Breedlove argue . . . (Chap. 9)
**Forrest:** That's not Breedlove. That's Witherspoon.

**Student:** Oh, I thought it was Breedlove.
**Forrest:** Oh, no. Breedlove would be much more religious. She probably wouldn't even have talked with Jamestown. But there are a lot of connections between Jamestown and Witherspoon. They were both men on the run. They were both individualists, quite arrogant and purposeful. Jamestown would be something of a kind of a figure, I suppose, for Nathaniel. He's something like Guitar in relation to Toni Morrison's Milkman.

The argument between Jamestown and Witherspoon also is somewhat like the implicit argument that is going on in *Invisible Man* between Booker T. Washington and W. E. B. Du Bois. In the first chapter of that novel, the invisible man gets in trouble there at the battle royal by saying "social equality." It stops everything. He goes back to "social responsibility." This would certainly have had an influence and, in our time, the argument between Martin Luther King and Malcolm X would be there too. But I want to take it to another level. What I wanted to do with eloquence on paper was to go beyond Malcolm or Martin Luther King or any of them. I have the arrogance to think I can do that on paper. I can never match them as talkers. I would not even try. But with great respect for Dr. King I think I have to have the faith that I can do things that these eloquent men couldn't do. I have the benefit of history. I have the benefit of other literatures that I can bring in there, whereas in an orally-delivered argument, you would not have the time to do that. You wouldn't have the audience to do that.

**Cawelti:** Would you say that there are echoes of Lincoln in Witherspoon's argument?

**Forrest:** The Lincoln section is very important to all of this. There you have an attempt to play with the agony of the man, even his looks. And to play with the myth of Lincoln and the mystery. They are connected.

**Student:** Did it help you to have Morrison's endorsement for your book?

**Forrest:** I think Morrison was almost as unknown as I was at the time. It wouldn't have been much help to have her name on the book then. She was very helpful in getting me published. As to marketing it, I was benefitted by two things. One was that Ellison wrote the introduction. His introduction and Saul Bellow's endorsement came in the same day. Then I got a terrific review from Anatole Broyard in the daily *New York Times*. We used all of that. There was never any thought that it would sell very much. To some degree, it was a benefit that Random House saw this as yet another affirmative action thing, to help them get through this period. They didn't think that black writing would be around long, at the time. It is just like black studies departments. The idea was in many places. "Let's get them through this. They are not going to last." There was no idea of investing in my talent by Random House, though Morrison believed in it. Ellison's introduction was more important to me for his opinion rather than his influence on sales. I just hoped that it would sell enough and people would get interested a little bit, so I would begin to develop an audience. I never had any interest in being popular, a best-selling commercial writer.

One danger with things in this country is that anything that has any credibility to it and yeast to it is soon going to be commercialized and lose its effectiveness. Much of the genius in Afro-American life has already been taken off, commercialized, and marketed. It's always a struggle to recreate it and give some originality to it. That was what be-bop did with jazz. As a serious artist, I can't get too concerned with the commercialization of Malcolm X, but I do connect it with what we have done with Lincoln and other figures. There's death, there's assassination, and there's canonization and then there's destruction and commercialization. It will probably take writers and historians many years to really get some leverage on Malcolm. I thought one of the problems with the movie was that it down-played the over-arching power in his life of Elijah Muhammad. I knew Muhammad fairly well. He was nobody's fool. An encounter between the two probably was like a very charismatic politician running into a master precinct leader.

**Student:** What new writers are you most interested in?
**Forrest:** I find myself increasingly going back to the writers that originally moved me. I very seldom find any new ones. One would be Rita Dove. I like her work a lot. I am always looking for those writers who will energize me because I am trying to fill each page with a certain turbulence and ecstacy and intelligence. I'm still particularly excited by the Russian writers, especially Dostoyevsky. Recently I've been transforming a verse play into a novel of voices with lots of monologues, and for that reason, I have been reading a lot of poetry. What I read depends a lot on what I am working on. If I am working on something where there is a lot of dialogue, then I will turn to plays. I am very fascinated by a lot of O'Neill and Archibald MacLeish, for instance.

**Student:** Are you bothered that your books haven't become best-sellers?
**Forrest:** Not really. I can't be bothered about that. All I can worry about is trying to see if I can write a great American novel. Northwestern University has been kind enough to give me a job so I can buy a decent meal and take my wife out occasionally and buy a good bottle of bourbon. My tastes are quite simple. Cawelti here has said some nice things about my work and that means a lot. The point is that writing means everything to me, since I am a person who is drawn to seek and project in an ultimate way some sense of order in life. I'm very drawn to the life of this chaotic and crazy country, but the one place where I can get some leverage on this is in writing. In situation after situation, when I have been involved in churches, in bars, in love affairs,

in all kinds of things, I was always sort of swept away. Writing is the one place where I can project this inner and outer chaos and transform it into something different. I didn't mean to sound as arrogant as I must have sounded earlier when I said I was trying to do better than Dr. King. I could never preach with these guys, but I can do something on paper, using their work as a spring-board. I also admire the great jazz musicians, but I couldn't play any instrument. I took piano for about 5 or 6 years and can't play a tune. But I do seem to have a good ear for what is going on in music and taking that and making that into something else. No, you may not be able to do all these things, but if you are a writer, you can use these sources for transformation into something else. Finally a writer has to be a crazy blend of a person who is arrogant and at the same time quite humble.

I've been lucky to have a great heritage, that of African American culture and I have benefited from that. It was a tremendous heritage and this heritage of literature, both black and western stood in my favor. But I have to transform all of this into something else to mean anything. As I once told my father, it saved my life. I would be over there is skid row or probably waiting for a drink if I weren't a writer. Literature can give you an ennobling sense of yourself and lift you up and save you sometimes, even though when you actually meet writers you may think they are mean little beasts until you read their work!

**Student:** Do you feel it is important to write about the past and the implications of history?

**Forrest:** Sure. It is important and it also is important to get past it. Because, you can get so overwhelmed by history, you can end up like one of Faulkner's characters, like Hightower, for example. There is a danger of becoming entrapped in the past and I think Morrison sees this. There's a problem, of course, with Black Americans and with what other Americans know about their past. A lot of it hadn't been recorded. A lot had been subordinated and left out of history books and literature and so on. On the other hand, you can get so trapped in going back, you don't do any new reinspection of the past. You sort of echo it. You get so involved in it that you can't free yourself. Blacks needed to do this, for sure and we all need to be aware that part of America's heritage is the slave past. My history is your history. Your history is my history. At the same time, you can be so entrapped by it that you don't go on. That's the great thing with the jazz musicians. People like Ellington,

Armstrong, Billie Holiday, Charlie Parker faced all kinds of vicious insults
and racism, yet look at the music they produced. Right in the face of it.

**Student:** Which Dostoyevsky novels do you like?
**Forrest:** *The Brothers Karamazov* and, of course, *Crime and Punishment* and
*Notes from Underground.* Dostoyevsky's sense of struggle going on within the
embattled soul I found to be instrumental for my own dealing with the divisions in the African-American soul. Dostoyevsky also had the sense that a
people can have a special mission. You've got that in the Civil Rights
Movement and a lot of people felt, certainly King and others did, that something special had happened to us here that could be a great service to the
country. Dostoyevsky was very much aware of how the Old Testament Jews
were transformed into a new kind of people through their suffering; this was
recombined in his imagination with the stories in the Gospel of the New
Testament.

There is also his interest in family life of all kinds, certainly a compelling
force in my writing. On another level, although I was quite influenced by
Ellison, I wanted to stake out my own territory. He didn't do very much with
family life, per se. For no matter how much the younger writer might admire
the older one, he or she must find ways of getting around that lion or lioness
of a literary consciousness and then you have to discover new ways in which
the older writer didn't approach the experiences of life. . . . It's as if you were
coming here to Lexington and all of you have heard about the strengths in
each of the performances at local Baptist churches here. And you want to
experience each one . . . and you discover that they have a great choir over at
this one . . . at another church you find that there is great preaching to experience each Sunday . . . so you know what's going on at Ellison's church, you
know what's going on in Baldwin's church, at Morrison's church, now I've got
to show you, reveal to you what is unique at Forrest's church. Just as we could
never confuse Billie Holiday with Sarah Vaughn, nor Ella Fitzgerald (that
great trinity of female singers); so too, I would hope that you would discover
the specialness of my work, in Forest County.

**Student:** As Kenneth Warren points out in his article, *There Is a Tree* has
become a different book because of the "Transformation" section. Could you
tell us the process you went through to finally end up with the novel as we
now read it, because that was added later?

**Forrest:** The "Transformation" section relates to the novel in many ways. There are several sermons in the novel, such as the sermonette of M. C. Browne, when he talks about his love of Jesus. I want to tell you a story about this. Browne is the boy who is beaten to death by his father because he is wearing a dress. Some time ago national public television approached Toni Morrison and requested that her work be used within the context of a gospel fest showcase, in Chicago. She suggested my work instead. They called me and I offered certain sections from all the works. The television producers decided on M. C. Browne's sermonette. A minister, who was scheduled to read the section, called me about 6 o'clock one morning. "Brother Forrest, I want to find out what is the meaning of this passage." I said, "Well, read it just as you would the Old Testament." He was sort of knocked back by that. What else could I have said? I might as well be arrogant. The weird thing about it all was the selection of this particular passage—given all the homophobia around. Black church people are as guilt of this as anybody else—despite the vital presence of gays at the heart and soul of some of the very best gospel singing.

But that is one of the sermonettes. There is also a sermon or sermonette which Hattie Breedlove Wordlaw delivers to Nathaniel. Someone asked earlier about the Vision section. That is presented as a kind of incantation—like a sermon. These all relate to the sermon that Pompey c.j. Browne (no relative of M. C.'s) gives in the "Transformation" section. Sweetie Reed's letter is very much in keeping with Lincoln and L.B.J. and the destruction of the leader. I can get a little bit more subtle on it, but that was the basic idea. I feel fully confident that the parts hang together—old with new. But I should leave that for the critics to say.

**Student:** Here's the book under cover and on the shelves, but you have an opportunity to modify it.
**Forrest:** That's right. And again I stole something from Faulkner, this idea of putting something in later. I remember telling Toni Morrison about the additions (after she had been my editor for my first three novels). She said that she sometimes wished she had a chance to do something a little more with *The Bluest Eye.*

**Cawelti:** Clearly one reason why you did that is that a new edition was coming out from Another Chicago Press. You might want to tell them about that.

**Forrest:** Well, Another Chicago Press is the kind of thing that gives you hope in this country, since this publisher is interested in bringing out quality books, instead of commercial smash-hits. That's the genius of this country in a way. The rise of independent publishers has become quite attractive. Now even the university presses in several places are publishing fiction. My publisher for the paperbacks and initially for *Divine Days*, Lee Webster, with Another Chicago Press, has been in the field for the last twelve years. He had learned of my work through his professor at UIC, Michael Anania. Webster decided if he ever did get involved in publishing he would make certain that my books were brought back out in paperback. All of my novels were out of print when Webster approached me about bringing the novels out, which were originally acquired by Toni Morrison when she was senior editor at Random House. We had of course Ellison's introduction to *There Is a Tree*. Toni Morrison again came to my rescue and wrote the introduction for *Two Wings to Veil My Face*. Mr. Cawelti was so kind to give my readers an excellent map of *The Bloodworth Orphans*.

   With Faulkner and all the stuff that was happening during the '20s with the jazz age and with literature, there has been a great tradition of experimentation and I wanted to keep that alive in my work. I am glad to see small presses like ANC coming along, because the commercial presses are so corrupt that all they want to do is cook books and photographic books and they are not open to experimentation. Even in my last novel, *Divine Days*, I was out there, looking for a publisher. Webster was the only one that would take it on, at the time. Of course, the manuscript was 1,829 pages . . . and yet there was a time in this country when if some writer came along, an adventurous, first-rate editor would have taken this manuscript on. Once *Divine Days* was published and got marvelous reviews from all the quarterlies, there was a fire and perhaps 75 copies of the novel were smoke-damaged; they were all in my publishers' basement. *Divine Days* had practically sold out the initial run of 1,500 copies. When that disaster occurred, we were able to get Norton interested in bringing the novel out (through my literary agent, Faith Childs). They brought the book out in hardback in July 1993, and they brought out the paperback in January 1995.

**Student:** One of the questions this class has touched on this semester was the problem which black critics had with William Styron's *The Confessions of Nat Turner*. This relates to the whole problem of crossing the color line in fiction.

Do you think there ought to be a sort of territorialization of fiction and that certain people are more qualified to write about certain subjects and be considered credible?

**Forrest:** I would expect that well-trained, well-educated black critics would bring something to the table and would unearth dimensions of both black and white novels that haven't been received before. That's what the rise of another people can do in the democracy and the laboratory of this country. Just as I would expect that women will tell us things, and indeed good sensitive feminist critics are doing this as well. However, I don't think it has to be a female critic or a black critic who can read sensitively. In other words the influence of sensitive women, if I am a good male critic, will enlighten me, so that I can look at texts by women and others in a new way. One hopes a kind of enlightened democracy can happen at this table, because of the diversity of the people here. Ultimately, as Morrison has shown, women can write about hunting scenes and any other kind of scenes. There's Joyce Carol Oates writing about boxing, for example. I believe in enlightened and sensitive, but tough-minded and open, criticism. I don't care, in the long run, for all these critical camps. They are camps. They have their limits. After awhile, you have all the women talking in a certain way; all the blacks talking, all the Hispanics talking a certain way. The danger is that you lose the sense of the daring possibility of the American experience and also the arrogance of my ambition. You know, Morrison has said herself that she's not always going to agree with everything that blacks and women say about her work. That's good. Diversity is all to our group health and our national truth.

**Student:** But isn't that more the ideal than the truth? In most universities, they shy away from someone black writing about some white author, and they shy away from males writing about female writers. I find that a lot of times they shy away from white critics writing about black writers. I see a bit more leniency there than someone black coming in and writing about a lot of white writers. Particularly when there are no black characters in a book.

**Forrest:** I guess we have to go through all of this, as a country in process. But I think we try to maintain two things. You want to have a rich production by every new group. Gays, for example, have a lot to add to the richness of culture. I teach Baldwin a lot. But I do think we need good gay critics who can bring a certain perspective to many of his novels. Much as I often teach *Another Country* and have come to admire it in many ways, there is a sense you really do need a gay sensibility to deal with a lot of that novel. However, I think it's important that having said that, I'm not going to stop teaching that novel and becoming more and more open to a gay sensibility in dealing with it. In the long run, it's how much you are willing to open your imagination up to the different sensibilities that are American. Yet, at the same time, we need to talk about what it means to be an American. That's the best part of Tennessee Williams. That is the best part of Ellison and Morrison, the best of Bellow, for instance. It is not only what it means to be Jewish, but how we find out what it means to be Jewish also has to lot to do with the way Jews have opened up the consciousness of this country. We are all part Jewish too. Certainly to be an American intellectual, you must be a Jew. That's all to the good. Now we are discovering that to be an American intellectual, you must be part black and maybe even discover you are part black. Later on we will see the influence of this, as we are seeing the way women are opening up our consciences. That is the great thing about the being an American right along with all the drive-by shootings and corruption in politics and all that.

**Student:** When you were talking about the destruction and resurrection of America, is it a matter of democracy or capitalism or what?

**Forrest:** Well, much of the corruption could be traced to capitalism. Look at the slave heritage, the auctions . . . so much of the economy was based in slavery. At the same time, the other side of it is the American genius in making things. There's a wizardry really in creating things with such power and invention. We've got some very bad schools here, but we've got wonderful universities. Look at all the Americans who win a Nobel prize every year for scientific exploration. That is part of the oneness of experimentation. What we are doing in science and space and so on, and that is possible in time with our literature and possible with our art. I'm not a Marxist, but we have a problem with America. It is very hard for us because along with the freedom of the laboratory and the spirit, there is the excess we get into of commercialization and it has tainted our values. It is hard for us, maybe because we are very young as a nation, to learn a kind of balance, a mean.

**Cawelti:** I think we are at the end of our time. Thank you, Leon Forrest.

# Angularity:
# An Interview with Leon Forrest

Keith Byerman / 1995

From *African American Review* 33.3 (Summer 1999), 439–50. © 1999 by
Keith Byerman. Reprinted by permission.

**Byerman:** Since we're in Chicago, I'd like to focus for a moment on the
importance of the city to your work. Especially with *Divine Days*, and to
some extent your other works, the setting is very specific. Could it be set
someplace else?

**Forrest:** I don't know, because Chicago is the city that captures this kind of
rowdy spirit that, it seems to me, has been missing so much from African
American letters. This blend of the sacred and the profane seems to me to be
so much a part of the Northern experience, particularly a city like Chicago
with its great possibilities of going for broke. It's a hustler's town. You can
make a comeback after falling, and people will let you up. It's not bound up
by class differences in the black community the way other cities are. The idea
of open-ended possibility in Chicago of the black community is really, to
some degree, true of the muscularity of Chicago in a general way; in other
literatures, it's mellow. Because of that, my fiction seems to me to be set
uniquely in a kind of Chicago, though I always call it Forest County work.
The specific things—barbershops, bars, and churches—you can find those
anyplace, but I hope they would have a certain Chicago character to them.

**Byerman:** One of the things you mention in *Relocations of the Spirit* is the
range of writers who have come from Chicago, who are associated with
Chicago—Lorraine Hansberry, Robert Hayden, Cyrus Colter, Gwendolyn
Brooks. Do you think there's something that these writers have in common
that has to do with the city?

**Forrest:** First of all, Hayden didn't come from Chicago—I just mention Hayden
as a favorite writer—and Hansberry was a little too neat for the ethos of
Chicago. Brooks is an outsider, and Colter is a transplanted guy from Indiana.

92

It's really Bellow who is close to the outlandishness of Chicago, the sense of the hustler's town, the role of certain kinds of tricksters, the great humor of it. I think I'm more in that kind of tradition, much more than I would be to the tradition of another transplant, Richard Wright. (Laughter.)

**Byerman:** I want to ask you about the idea of the voices in *Divine Days*. One of the things that struck me in reading through the book is that, while the characters are very different and their stories are very different, their voices seem to have a lot in common; that is, there seems to be this piling on of language and the playing with language (all the puns and other types of word play). Many of the significant voices in the text have this in common. Is there some sense in which they're all simply your voice?
**Forrest:** Oh, no, not at all. I mean, I hope that each has his/her own coinage, but I obviously am attracted to certain kinds of characters who evolve in my artistic imagination who are great talkers, and there is a kind of tradition of an orchestrated oral tradition, in which you start off with A, move to C, move to E, and then come back and pick up B and D. That has to do with the way jazz moves, and the folk sermon and just general storytelling. But having said that, that would be part of the ethos of the race as I was seeing it, projecting. The voices—in terms of their dictions, the tonalities, the specifics of the kinds of stories they tell—are very different. For instance, a character like Gracie the barmaid is telling this long story about her son who was killed in Korea and who was, strangely and perhaps even intriguingly, bisexual. That's quite different than a character like Reverend Rupert, who talks about the meaning of the spiritual moment and takes it to the mountain tops. Both are great talkers, I guess, but very different.

**Byerman:** So you would see these characters as, in some sense, jazz instruments or jazz voices, each interacting with the others but having its own tonality?
**Forrest:** Jazz is the one art form that we all know so well. Often the great instrumentalist or ensemble creations are orchestrated just as sermons are orchestrated; they start off with one thing, and you constantly expand and improvise. My characters do the same thing. But it seems to me that what you're talking about is a major kind of outline or feature of the ethos of African American oral tradition and, again, it is highlighted in jazz. I find it going on in characters who are very different from each other. Obviously that

would be the role for the scholar to find out: Why that is or why that isn't true, or how universal it is.

**Byerman:** One of the questions I want to get to eventually is the question of history and why one looks back at the story. First, do you think that such variety of voices and such creativity in voices—because I think that's part of what I'm getting at, this play with language and so forth—continues to exist today? That is, you set the story in 1966 in barbershops and bars, spaces that permit such expression. Do you think that it continues to exist as part of an ethos today?

**Forrest:** It would take a cultural anthropologist, I suppose, to get to the precision of that. I would say it does exist; at least its layers continue. For instance, there's the whole tradition that I'm not really up on of rap talk and rap music; there would be the whole influence of the drug culture; there would be greater emphasis now on a political language; there would be the influence of keen interest in Africa—all of these things are added to it. Meanwhile, the old base is still there. All the things that are part of signifying, dozens playing, tall tales, blues. I don't probably do enough in the novel on the whole impact of the urban blues and the commercialization of it in the community. So I would say that, if anything, the layers of the talk continue to expand, some things less important than others, but the old layers are still there with the new ones as well.

**Byerman:** Does this notion of the layers have something to do with a term that you use frequently in *Relocations* and elsewhere—the notion of *angularity*— because it's clear that you don't mean simply something like point of view. What does that term mean, and how does it apply to your work?

**Forrest:** Well, it's the way things have a spiraling kind of effect. I say orchestrated, but things will move in a variety of directions, and then often times, when the best speakers find a wholeness . . . I'm very much interested in that because I always am very fearful of any kind of formula in writing. The fact that one person develops a kind of talk in one way, and then another in another way, orchestrates an angular involvement in talk and speech patterns—that is very important to me. So that might well be the effect, for instance, with Rupert, who is a minister; he's still very close to a kind of orchestrated, church-based formula that affects him even when he's talking in a secular way. Now someone like Gracie the barmaid, who's talking about her son, she's not limited by that; she can bring anything, any kind of diction in and use any kind of structure in her talk. Rupert is so bound by the church that, when the two of them are in dialogue, another kind of angularity happens that's open-ended too. He's from the medley of preachers and so is always trying to get back to certain things. So, again, you have a mix here. Now, the other thing that connects the two is this mix of the sacred and the secular or the sacred and the outrageous always coming together.

**Byerman:** Can the sacred be outrageous?
**Forrest:** Oh, yes indeed. It always is at base. There is this one Bible story, a lot of preachers pick up on it, and that's the story of Josea and Gorma. This man marries a woman who is reported to be a prostitute, and it becomes a metaphor, in the prophetic tradition, of God's willingness to forgive, because Josea was willing to forgive Gorma, who was in a life of prostitution. The idea was that the Israelites along the way had picked up all of these profane ways and had prostituted themselves to the traditions and so on of the people who had surrounded them—Arabs, the Egyptians, and so on—and God was willing to forgive them. But at the base of this is the story of a man who's been cuckolded. So, you're taking this on a serious leap of faith: Josea was made a fool of, you know, and he forgave his wife. How many times does she have to be caught with somebody? So a lot of the stories that we've come to think of as holy stories in the Bible and other places really have a comical base to them. That's what I'm always looking for, and to some degree that humanizes me.

But I was going to go back a bit to your other question, because maybe the comparison would be the relationship of *Invisible Man* to *Divine Days*, in terms of another book that's full of talk and voices and so on, and then to see that I'm in that tradition and then to see how I've expanded that tradition with more voices. And that would be the difference of about fifteen years or twenty years of setting. So, again, my point would be that this stuff expands. In *Song of Solomon* you get a muted sense of the expansion in the scene in the barbershop that's so wonderful in there. There's only about ten pages, but I could never do it in ten pages; I'd have to have thirty.

**Byerman:** Okay. That leads to the question of why *Divine Days* in its published form has to be 1,135 pages long, and in its manuscript form has to be 1,829 pages long. Why did it require so much space to tell the story?

**Forrest:** Well, because it's so Divine. (Laughter.) I don't know. We don't think of tightness when we think of the great major novels, and that's obviously what I was after. How well I succeeded is another question. But no one called Joyce in to ask why didn't he cut *Ulysses* down to 750 pages or so, why didn't he cut it to 300.

**Byerman:** But *Divine Days* is longer than that, half again as long. It's three times as long as a Faulkner novel.
**Forrest:** Yeah, sure. That's pretty good. Well, those are just people that you've got to beat, so you've got to see if you can box them in the long-distance run. I was very much after the fact that so and so had written a novel of this length, and I'd need something much larger, much grander, more voices to get up on the shelf and compete with these people. I come from a tradition that the writer should really think about writing the Great American Novel, so I said, well, I better write the Great World Novel.

**Byerman:** Then you do have the sense of seeing those writers as, in some sense, benchmarks.
**Forrest:** Benchmarks and active competitors. They're dead, but the books are just as alive as they can be to me. The other thing is that I thought I needed this kind of length for sustained character development, which nobody does anymore. I won't call any names, but even the writers that we like most . . . there's rarely any kind of really sustained character development over a long period of time, going back in time and forward and seeing these characters cast in different waters—temptation, honor, wonder, and all that. I felt that it certainly would take that kind of length to do it, but I didn't have any problem with it. And, then, I was having so much fun with the novel. It's not like when you're a kid and you have a ring that you're shooting marbles in, and it's a small ring, you know. I said, "Hell, this ring, the whole block belongs to me, and these marbles, and let's see what happens. Ideas are coming up and jokes, and this and that, put this in and, oh, don't forget this." Or someone would tell me something and I would be actively working to transform it.

You know, interestingly enough, none of the reviewers complained about the length; they all mentioned it, but none complained about it. I have a sense that more people have probably gotten deeper into this novel than any of my other novels, and the other novels are much shorter.

**Byerman:** One model that occurs to me that you haven't mentioned in terms of openness and vastness is Thomas Wolfe, and I'm wondering if he is part of the background here in any sense?

**Forrest:** I was never a very big Wolfe fan for some reason or other. I was much more with Faulkner and the Russian writers. I've thought more and more about the Russian writers in the last ten years or so because it seems to me that you can get this expansiveness of a broad range of culture there, many layers of it, the conflict of it, the grandness of it, and the great tribulation of life, and that's a big important ingredient to me—and the humor that you see with Ellison, that was a big influence. So, you know, I actively sought ways in which I am connected with these writers and then how I might try to see what I could do on their turf.

**Byerman:** Do you see this work as going beyond those writers then?

**Forrest:** Well, that would be for someone else to say; that I don't know. Someone had mentioned about this being an African American *War and Peace* and I said, well, the only connection that I have on that level to Tolstoy is the fact that we share the same first name. Well, almost. Anyway, these are the people that I was actively inspired by and actively thinking about how I might compete with, the great ones, of course.

**Byerman:** The other connection with Wolfe, in some ways, is the apparent autobiographical element in the text. That is, Joubert in some ways seems like a young Leon Forrest—in the army, working in a bar, doing local journalism, and so fourth. In what sense and in what ways is this autobiographical, or is this just a starting point?

**Forrest:** It's just a starting point. But I'll use anything if I can make it work. A lot of things have happened to me that I can't use because I can't get the distance from them or the passion into them. The bar seemed the perfect place. I had worked in bars for years. But the people in the novel are only faintly based on people I knew. I stayed away from the bar scene perhaps for twenty years before I tried to write about it. I sat in the park one summer and just started taping memories, different memories of bar scenes that I had had. And things were just springing up that I thought I'd forgotten about. Then I would sit down at the typewriter and work from that tape. Being away that long I had forgotten enough to provide a springboard to improvise. So sure, I'll use anything I can, but soon enough, of course, the many characters I'm dealing with have to have their own lives and integrity, and that's where I've got to give over to them my imagination to evolve that.

**Byerman:** How do you see *Divine Days* as relating to the earlier novels? The first three novels work as a kind of trilogy. How do you see this book, set in the same place more or less, with some of the same characters, as relating to those earlier books?

**Forrest:** The setting goes back and forth in the South and North, and that's certainly true in the first three novels. Hopefully there is a leap in my own artistic growth, and *Divine Days* has a lot of comedy and humor of all kinds that is not pervasive in the first three novels. Also there is this kind of sustained development of several major characters that you don't have much of in the first three novels. The first three novels had a fundamental religious base to them, and the seriousness of the religious and spiritual question in my work may well be the reason that I've had such problems developing sustained critical attention. These issues are there in *Divine Days* for sure, even in the title, though it is also comical, but there are also a lot of other things going on there.

**Byerman:** As a reader of your own work, with the perspective of four novels, do you see yourself in some sense as a religious writer in that spiritual issues are at the center of what you talk about?

**Forrest:** Yeah, because I don't want to contradict myself. Ford, you know, is sort of a profane character who manipulates a religion ultimately. Of the other two main characters, Sugar-Groove is apparently taking a kind of spiritual turning the last years of his life, and then Imani, Joubert's girlfriend, has all kinds of spiritual quandaries about her relationship to Africa and her relationship to her past and family, and these are spiritual issues from in her psyche. But in *Divine Days* there's also, more than in any of the other novels, the idea of the comedy of faith. You get some of that in *Finnegans Wake* and elsewhere in Joyce, and many other writers play with that. At base, even the most religious questions have a kind of humorousness or even comical undergirding.

**Byerman:** Ford in this novel seems to be played in part for comic purposes. In the earlier work, he was a kind of trickster figure, among other things. The angle I want to take is why you would give him a name that would read so easily as W. D. Fard, of Black Muslim tradition.

**Forrest:** There's the actual closeness in both stories, both the story that we know of Fard and my Ford, to manipulation and mystery—the intrigue and perhaps even a sense of the closeness that so many religious figures have to the magician and to the trickster. They look alike, for instance, and so on. But that's why, of course, the Muslims always play around with the idea that Fard was really God incarnate. So then I take Ford (and the tradition) a step further and have him a hermaphrodite who keeps coming back again and again. Of course, we only see manifestations of his maleness. He's a stud. He's wearing all these different masks, and actually what we have left of Fard is a series of masks of interpretations. So, that's a base—Prophet Divine, Prophet Jones, Daddy Grace—a kind of history of the world, a trickster, some African tricksters. All of this and more constitute the stock that went into the material of Ford.

**Byerman:** A question about one of the essays in *Relocations*, specifically the one on Elijah Muhammad: One of the things that struck me was precisely that you chose Elijah rather than Malcolm X, who everybody is writing about. What is it about Elijah Muhammad that caught your attention?
**Forrest:** Well, first of all, I knew him, and I didn't know Malcolm. Second, as you're indicating, so much is written about Malcolm, so why do another one? And then it seemed to me, as I guess I indicated in the essay, that in this country there's a tendency to look more to Kennedy than to Johnson, and a lot of times these characters who are less known publicly and seem even to be secretive are really quite fascinating on a one-to-one basis and in small groups. That was certainly true with the perception I had of Elijah, and of course he was at the real fundamental base of the movement, not Malcolm. I thought that, in writing about him, I would approach it with a kind of comic base, so that there was a certain kind of humor there, you know, because that's been missing in these deliberations. As I was telling my wife one night after I had gone over there—and I quote this in the book—he said, "Oh, Napoleon meets Napoleon." (Laughter.) I wish people who were seriously involved in biographies would look to some of these things because it would be wonderful if we knew much more about Mayor Daley #1, or Richard J., who for all intents and purposes, was not much of a talker, yet this guy knew more about power and could manipulate power and knew an awful lot more about human nature than any of these highly articulate people. So Elijah would be in that tradition.

**Byerman:** One of my reads of what's going on in *Relocations* is that you discuss a number of people who could be seen as reinventing something. Was Elijah Muhammad in some sense that kind of person, one who takes something that is out there and remakes it?

**Forrest:** He epitomized it. I don't know if I quote this in the book but I was telling a grandson of his about *There Is a Tree*, and he said, "Well, that's an intriguing title. Tell the old man that and he'll pick it up."

(Laughter.) And it makes sense: He was an artist; he'd steal anything and make it into something else. A better answer is what Joubert does with this whole thing of improvisation: He goes on the other side of the bar and starts taking these spare parts that nobody wants and puts them together like an automobile maker in Detroit. All that is invention, the inventive person in the African American context and maybe in others as well. The Bop musicians, for instance, were so damned sour on current music that they wanted to try something new. It wasn't just to play a music that the white folks couldn't copy; it was a kind of cockiness of the artistic personality. I don't like this old stuff that's gone before. Well, Elijah did that, too. He picked up a little of this and a little of that, and soon enough he had a mythology. As I mention, blacks need their own mythology to challenge the white man's mythology.

Christianity, as a white man's religion—Dr. King took it and made it a black religion. But all of this is part of reinvention, and bringing in some Islam, and the other thing that is a part of the innovative personality. It's very interesting how Elijah's movement was really very old-fashioned, respectful, very Southern, gracious toward women, chauvinistic, too, of course: taking care of your own property and standing up for what you are, and the way they dress, particularly the women; even taking something like the damned bow tie and making it into some kind of statement. Isn't this the messenger that delivers the message? (Laughter.) All of that is going into this cauldron, you know. And he shaped it. Some of it he understood—a lot of it he probably didn't. Malcolm never did any of that.

**Byerman:** One of the things that struck me about your essay is that, in some sense, Elijah becomes more central than Malcolm. Malcolm may have been able to articulate things much more dynamically, but Elijah was the one back there doing all the work.

**Forrest:** Well, that's like Paul; he was a much more dynamic speaker than Jesus. He extended the faith. There is a lot of that idea of the triad of leadership. Again, Ellison is helpful here: You've got the Founder and Bledsoe, and then you've got Homer Barbee. Barbee is the great explainer of the myth. It is often times the person who comes after what the founder has crafted who can be an even greater spokesman. He's been converted to it, and in some ways he may even love it more. He's more invested in it. By the time you've got the whole thing crafted, you begin to see some of the traps in it.

**Byerman:** Is there some way in which *Relocations* is—given this discussion— a way for you to create a tradition for yourself?

**Forrest:** I think that's a very thoughtful question. It may well be a little like how we've come to use *Shadow and Act* as an undergirding for *Invisible Man*. I wish I could say that about Baldwin's brilliant essays, but in his fiction that isn't true. I hear echoes in the two, and certainly the sensitive critic can hear more in the two works. I wish I had written in fiction the equivalent of my essay on Billie Holiday.

**Byerman:** Is there a fictional Billie Holiday in there somewhere?

**Forrest:** I don't think so, but she represents a kind of reverential base, source material that is there is many ways.

**Byerman:** What struck me about *Relocations* is that we have a long essay on Elijah and then at the end this long essay on Billie Holiday, and much of the language that you use in them is very similar. This whole notion of reinvention, of angularity even, comes across in the two discussions. Both persons seem to take a humble role (or attitude) for this great thing that they have become a part of. It struck me that in fact they have this sort of workman-like role of taking material that is out there and reinventing it and reshaping it into some- thing. And what turns out is something quite impressive, quite powerful. It seems that part of what you're doing is saying that's your background—you listen to them and you learn from them.

**Forrest:** Yeah. I guess you could say that. Just as Elijah took all these broken down parts of human beings that had been shattered by the world, discarded by whites and blacks, and made them into something—this shiny car—Billie took the men who discarded her and remade them. That was her art.

**Byerman:** She remade the clichéd songs.

**Forrest:** That's right. Holiday, and many other persons I was fascinated with as a young person—Dylan Thomas and Charlie Parker, for instance—were chaotic across the board. But on stage they somehow or other were able to make something that is so transcendent and so wonderful and tremendous; they were in a lot of control. Yet they were controlled by the forces that would destroy them in their offstage lives. The other thing is that they were such enormously needy people. That was not true of Elijah.

**Byerman:** Is that a model of the artist for you—taking these bits and pieces that others might disregard and shaping them into something?
**Forrest:** That's right. And it's particularly true of things the white world has discarded and the black world has discarded or underplayed. I'm still forcing the idea or pushing the idea of the importance of religious or spiritual experiences. And I'm about the only black writer who is still doing it. Baldwin did it for awhile and got tired of it. It is at the very nerve of the ethos.

**Byerman:** Back to this idea of reinvention—is there no true originality, just the remaking of things?
**Forrest:** Well, it's a blend. I'm talking about the Renaissance, the music of Ellington or Billie—all of these things are a blend. The more layered they are, the greater the possibility for a projection that's closer to what we are and who we are as people. One of the sad things that has happened to blacks in the ghetto, particularly the younger people, is that they have cut themselves off from this idea of invention. They've sort of retreated into the haunts of inwardness or parochialism, and that's not the way to go. That's certainly not the way for an oppressed people to free themselves. You constantly need to make contacts with whatever it is that's perceived as the classical mode, whether it's in business or anything else. Engage it, first of all, and then refine it and change it in terms of your own needs. This is something we've known for a long time, but we have kind of cut ourselves off from it. The artists and the people that we respect most in the black community represent exactly what I'm talking about. They're willing to engage the broadest spectrum of our cultures and then combine it with what we have to make the new. If rap is ever going to go anyplace—and I'm not knocking rap, it may well go—but if it's ever going to do more than be a narcissistic expression, then it's going to have to do something like that. It's going to have to redefine itself, grow, expand, engage other worlds to have a definitive stamp on our conscious.

**Byerman:** Do you think that this notion of reinvention is, in some way, a kind of essence of African American culture? Is it what the culture means in some sense?

**Forrest:** Sure. What I'm talking about too is this will for improvisation and almost fitful effort. You never get a preacher preaching the same story of Job the same way on a particular Sunday over a career of say forty years in the pulpit. You deal with the chaos of life by using the imagination and taking old forms, like the story of Job, and reapplying them to the agony and wonder of the day-in and day-out year-in and year-out, generation-in and generation-out, and so on, story. And you never back off from any of that. I come up with something that's very specific about something that happens to blacks and then see how that connects up with what's been called a kind of classical experience of that in other literatures, other worlds, and then I draw the two together. That's part of how art is made.

**Byerman:** In your case, and perhaps more generally among African American writers, there's a strong emphasis on history and memory. Part of what I hear you saying is these are the materials we work with to create new works. Why set a novel in 1966, as opposed to 1996, and address the immediate questions?

**Forrest:** I wanted to capture a time in which the ethos of the characters and the ethos of the black community are coming through a period of transition. We really had come to believe that the Civil Rights Movement was about at an end around 1966, and so this is kind of coming between these two. Here's the Black Power period and, of course, that's a big quandary, and so Joubert is interested in it. He's very fascinated by the Movement—on the one hand by King —and yet he doesn't like the violence of the new groups because he feels that he knows enough about violence from the South to shun that. Some of the arguments in the bar have to do with this. He is in the scene in the bar when the Muslim comes in, and there is a big argument between them about this little boy, the kid in the shop, this drug addict. All these issues are around this issue of war and peace and around aggression and violence, I guess you could say. These are the issues that run at the heart of a novel. 1966 represents an era, a time, but it's also useful to think about the way these issues are dealt with in the book and of our situation today.

**Byerman:** Does the past then give us some perspective on the present?
**Forrest:** I hope so. There's another past of Joubert, and there's the past of Sugar-Groove and his past with his father. And so there are at least three, and perhaps more, ways of plunging into the immediate past and then the deeper past to make sense of patterns where they are.

**Byerman:** What does the pattern amount to, do you think?
**Forrest:** I guess the pattern would be how to find sources of invention to work through, to transcend the chaos and also to devise ways in which you constantly are finding some angle of vision, finding within yourself some spiraling power to make your life richer and more human. One of the problems with someone like Imani, for instance, is that she is trapped in the past and can't seem to get beyond it. She's right to tell Joubert about the importance of the past, but she is so locked into it, whereas some of the other characters like Sugar-Groove, who is interested in the past, don't know how to define it. Of course, Ford manipulates the past more than any-one else. So the thing would be to be wary of people who are constantly talking about what they've learned from the past, the ones who are going to absorb us in that because they, often times, are making profit off of it and aren't showing us the way to a future.

**Byerman:** Do you think that searching for those patterns might inform us about the present? Is that a special function for black artists today, or is that more general?
**Forrest:** Yes, but it's a temptation for the writer to speak in too closely shaped didactic terms about this. This must be designed by the writer himself/herself, and it is clear to me that you must get lost in this material to find your way out, to some degree. Certain writers like to make a pattern and say we need to do this or that. I don't want to preach sermons. I would rather show characters and then, out of that, let the reader decide to "look at the blind alley this guy is going down." It suggests a way of constant improvisation, constantly trying to make new. That seems to me to be a healthy thing, a wonderful thing. When we do it, we do two things. One is to hold on fiercely to the anguish and grief of our heritage. That is something that we owe ourselves and the nation. The other thing is to see constantly how we can find ways of invention to deal with this anguish. But that's what the great sermons do . . . "You were Job, and now let's see how you can get out of your predicament."

**Byerman:** Let's move a little bit beyond your own work to some observations about what's going on with African American writers generally. First of all, do you see any patterns among the writers now, or is everybody sort of doing his or her own thing?

**Forrest:** Well, first of all you have about a half a dozen writers, male or female, who would be in their 50s through mid-60s who've established a good group of novels. These would be Gaines, Wideman, Morrison, and perhaps myself, and others. The point would be that we haven't had this before because, you know, it was only toward the end of Baldwin's life that he had a body of novels, and they are very uneven. We've had the one novelist all right, with perhaps six novels, but this is kind of unusual that you have so many writers, six or more . . . and we'll go on. Now the question will be how far we can go on beyond what we've done. And that will be the test of how sustained the quality of African American letters will be going into the new century. We're all at a kind of middle-level development. And maybe a little bit beyond that.

So the question would be, "What greatness is there for any of us?" We will see what we will see. August Wilson would be in this group as well. And then you have some very interesting poets like Michael Harper and Rita Dove, for instance, so it's really quite an impressive group. And, as I said, many are young enough to write what will be great works. African American letters at this point is the most exciting branch of American literature.

**Byerman:** One of the things that seems to be happening is that a number of writers of the generation that you're talking about have also been producing nonfictional works. There's Charles Johnson, you, Morrison, Gayl Jones (who is a little bit younger but nonetheless certainly a part). Ishmael Reed has been writing nonfiction all along. What is the compulsion do you think to write nonfiction as well as fiction?

**Forrest:** Ellison got very much intrigued by this. As much as Baldwin wanted to write a great novel, ultimately it was the essays that made his reputation. I think what drives the black writer is the fact of the immediacy of issues that so beleaguer us in fiction. This is true for those of us in it for the long haul; to deal with more abiding issues of life and death and racial crisis, we have to address these contemporary issues. We're also constantly asked, you know, "What about this? What about the O.J. trial?" All these things come up constantly in society, life, and there is also a need to do something about that.

Now there is also another kind of essay that many of the black writers are involved in, and that is the kind of essay that I hear you talking about when you ask what undergirds my work. There is a feeling for many of us writers that deconstructionists and the rest of them have missed the boat. We know something about society and culture and literature even though most of us don't have Ph.D.s and many of us don't have degrees at all. That's being avoided and not addressed by the people who are teaching literature, by the cultural theorists and others, and so that inspires another sort of essay. Then the other thing is all of us are back in the university now. So we've been taken over by this stuff; we teach all the time and want to show we know our stuff there as well. So, all of these things are a part of the drive.

**Byerman:** There seems to be some sense in which the writers have insights that we can trust, that aren't necessarily there even among the people who are observers of African American culture. I'm thinking of people like Cornel West and bell hooks. And there's some way in which, you know, even as good as their observations can be, there is a kind of perception that you have or Morrison has or Ellison has that seems to go beyond what it is that they are doing.

**Forrest:** And our drive is to say, "Yeah, but don't see this as something natural, you know, like they do with black athletes." Well that's where we then try to get heavy, and that's where we get into problems, too. There's a tradition of this in this country with Henry James, and Baldwin had read a lot of James and so had Ellison, and these are our two greatest black essayists in a way, I think. So, there is a tradition for that—of letters.

**Byerman:** What observations would you be interested in making about literary theory—that is, postmodernism, poststructuralism, and also the discussions that have been going on about multiculturalism? You express a view that deconstructionism somehow misses the boat, but would you say that more generally about theoretical approaches to black literature, the kinds of things that Gates and Baker and a number of other people are doing? How do you, as a writer as well as a teacher of literature, deal with these things, and how relevant do you see them as being?

**Forrest:** I read some of it, but I stay away from a lot of them because I think they can be very damaging to me as a creative writer, because the gauge is formulaic. I ultimately must, as an artist and novelist, not belong to anybody but the source material that's available to me when I'm trying to create. I must not belong to Europe, though I'm deeply influenced by Europe. I must not belong to Africa. I don't belong to the New Orleans creoles. I don't belong to the South Side. I don't belong to the woman's movement. I certainly don't belong to the Black Aesthetic. Yet, to some degree, I must deal with all of that. The way I deal with it best is to learn it. Anything else is reductionist.

**Byerman:** Is the artist finally then a kind of lonely individual?
**Forrest:** Sure, but that goes with the territory. That's what I bought into when I decided to go into this operating room. You can get so much more done in the novel and the literature when you're not staking out, "Well now, this is the audience, and I want to address this. I'm talking to women now."

**Byerman:** Do you see yourself as having a particular audience; that is, when you sit down to write, who do you expect to read what you're writing?
**Forrest:** This may sound naïve, but what I'm really dreaming for would be a group of serious African American readers; that would be my ideal audience. The other audience would be anyone who is interested in serious literature. I guess, in another way, I'm not all that obsessed with audience. Maybe that's why I don't sell anything. I kind of take the materials available to me and make something of them in a magical way with language and character transformation and so on. In other words, it's different from the performer who knows, "Now I may be very caught up in certain eccentricities or something, but I've got to get out there and entertain an audience tonight." A writer is working alone with his materials, hopefully finding things that will engage an audience, of course, but more than that, since fiction separates me from the playwright, who is not alone.

**Byerman:** I wanted to ask you about the whole idea of creative writing and creative writing classes. What value or purpose do you see in them? Can one become a good writer by taking creative writing classes?
**Forrest:** Not too many—a few, and with very good teachers. And those teachers don't necessarily have to be writers at all but people who are very sensitive to literary nuance and are willing to suggest ways in which the young writer can expand his talent and where he can go, people he can talk to, books he can read. But the main thing is that young writers become too

dependent on creative writing, and it becomes another crutch. And, ultimately, of course, all crutches must be taken from you.

**Byerman:** You're on your own and out there by yourself. First of all, what has
been your experience at Northwestern, a university that is considered to be,
in many ways, an elite institution where you have a relatively privileged group
of students? What is it like being an African American in such aninstitution?
**Forrest:** It's very lonely. My friend Allison Davis, to some degree, prepared
me for that because he was a friend for a little over eighteen years, and I used
to see him at the University of Chicago and so on. Your friends are few. Well,
to put it another way, for any academic most of your colleagues are out of
places in your specific area, and you're not going to get a lot of colleagues
who see the need for a very progressive, even radical agenda that is going to
transform this society to be a help to my people and to the poor and so on.
They all have their own disagreements with other blacks. All of this is exacer-
bated by the fact that you're the artist in the university, you know, probably
don't hold formal degrees, and you're looked upon as probably a quaint,
interesting outsider. It adds to the sense of being a minority within a minority within a minority. I would say, in the long run, maybe sometime early
next century, you will see black writers finding other ways to make a living
other than the university. Don't forget that I was thirty-six when I came to
Northwestern, so I had another life. And I think it's very dangerous for
people going from M.F.A. programs to teach because they haven't lived and
experienced, and they talk the same kind of babble, team-speak, and they all
sound alike. The creation of literature is always about risk taking.

**Byerman:** One of the things that isn't very specific in your work is your own
political views. That is, those are not really identifiable in terms of the work
that you do. Toni Morrison has, for example, made an effort to identify herself with certain issues, primarily outside of her fiction. What's the place of
politics in your world view, and in your personal experience? Do you see
yourself as a political person in any sense?
**Forrest:** Well, I'm a Chicagoan, and therefore by definition I'm a Democrat.
I suppose the thing I liked in Mayor Washington was that you had
Democrats, radicals, leftovers from the Civil Rights Movement, leftovers
from the nationalist period supporting him. I would call myself a kind of
"race" man. I always want to see how we can come up with techniques to

help survive and flourish in the society. So, if you're a socialist or you're an NAACP man, well that's all right too. We can work together because we try to see what we can do in the world today. And that's the thing that sort of bothers me, too; the Afrocentric movement has no place for expansion. I think that I am a political man, but I do not necessarily use the idiom. I don't have an overriding identification with politics and ideology of Africa. I have great identification with hard-struck humanity. I see a situation that is not particularly giving us any direction about what we must do. I would say that the way we can help Africa, as we have seen, would really be through the rise of a sophisticated black middle class that has the time and interest, perhaps in African art, to have a relationship with Africa that perhaps the Jews have with Israel. They're clear, the Jews, of their connections with Israel.

**Byerman:** The question is which Africa?
**Forrest:** That's exactly right. I have to always kind of pull back. Of course, there is political mayhem in *Divine Days* with some of these tricksters who are manipulating African art, too.

**Byerman:** Now for the question that always ends an interview: What are you working on?
**Forrest:** Well, I'm working on two things. One is a novel that would be composed of about five or six novellas. It's pretty experimental. It picks up some things on Joubert and some old things and, then, some very new things. I'm also working, and I may well have it in a few years, on another collection of essays. One thing about the essay that I did mention is that it allows you to take the spirals of ideas and then convert them into the essay form that you perhaps, at one time, thought might be good in a novel—an anecdote that didn't seem to go anywhere—and, of course, Naylor and Baldwin were very helpful with this, using anecdotes in essays. Those are the two things.

**Byerman:** Thank you for a great afternoon.

# The Yeast of Chaos:
# An Interview with Leon Forrest

Molly McQuade / 1995

From *Chicago Review* 41.2/3 (1995). © 1995 by Molly McQuade. Reprinted by permission.

For a writer, the ideal artistic community is made up of musicians, painters, a few writers—and a lot of people interested in the arts in a general way. I was drawn to the University of Chicago because I thought I would find that community there.

I lived in a building at 61st and Dorchester, right across from the university. Musicians and painters and writers lived in it with me. It was owned by an elderly Jewish woman who had been a Communist, though not a card-carrying one. She had all these wonderful records of Paul Robeson's. In the building there were a lot of political people and people of different races—Africans, Indians. I was hanging out, hanging around, meeting a wonderful group of people.

At the same time, I was trying to write. I was also working for a community newspaper and later for the Muslim paper *Muhammad Speaks*. I was teaching a creative writing class at Kennedy-King Junior College one day a week. I was taking classes at the University of Chicago.

That was a time of great chaos in my life, because I was trying to find my was as a writer. I had a lot of energy. I heard all those different voices and saw all those different lives and they all were struggling to achieve themselves. My problem was to make something out of this.

Chaos is very important to a writer—all of this life bubbling around, and you trying to get in there and take what you need from the material and then transform it into something.

You have to take what you can, then ultimately drift away from it in order to shape what you need. But initially there must be chaos, so that you can place your stamp on it. You must be attracted to it and not let it destroy you. And that's really a fight. In a lot of cases, chaos destroys writers, either through the destructive nature of the writer, or through addiction to the scene itself—the frantic people who take over your life and waste you, or alcohol, or drugs, or just you, running the streets to your detriment and ultimately becoming more of a talker than a writer, a priest of the bars.

The things that I loved in life and wanted to convert and transform into literature were themselves filled with the yeast of chaos. I might have been destroyed by the chaos I was so drawn to that I couldn't get a hold on it. And I couldn't get a hold on my own sort of discipline, either. There was a tension between discipline and chaos. My battles were between the flesh and the spirit; they were about the question of race, about the question of how to write out of a sensibility of oppressed people, about the fact that so many heroes of that drama were people filled with rage and chaos who eventually lost their lives in the struggle. And my battle was intensified by the fact that, in wanting to become a writer, I was joining a minority within a minority. Models were few, Ellison being one.

In the Irish and the Jewish cultures, a writer, an intellectual, was admired. In the black culture, no. This contributed to my chaos. I couldn't seem to finish anything. I couldn't finish school, I couldn't finish anything. It was awful. I had to develop a certain sturdiness, and it was touch and go whether I ever would.

I ended up at the University of Chicago because of an ambition I had, fostered in me by my parents and by my teachers in grade school and in high school.

My father was a bartender on the railroad. We were lower-middle-class. He was a self-made man, hypersensitive and high-strung. So it was kind of difficult to get to him. I wasn't tough enough to speak up to him. Daddy was absolutely certain that I was going to become a doctor—based on nothing!

My family had a lot of great storytellers, mostly my aunts and uncles. And my father used to come back from his railroad job with stories. He was a very engaging man, so he'd bring stories from jazz musicians as well as from the whites on the train who would talk to him. Daddy would also read a lot to me, and so would my mother. Because I was the only child of two only children, I was the pet of the family, I'd sit around and listen to people talk, and I would not break into the conversations of adults. Maybe I wanted to, but maybe I had the good sense not to!

They would read anything to me that they could get their hands on. My father would take books out of the library and read to me—books by

Zane Grey and so on. Until I was about nine, my great-grandmother lived with us, and I would read the Bible to her and with her. Later I was raised partly by a woman who lived with us all of my growing-up years. She was a spinster from Kentucky. She would read to me, and I would read to her. I also had the task after Mass of reading the Gospel and the Epistle to an invalid— an aunt on my mother's side, the Catholic side.

My father was interested in writing; he wrote songs and had two published. (He never made any money from them.) He had a very nice singing voice, kind of like an Irish tenor mixed in with the sound of the Ink Spots' Bill Kenney. He recorded some of his songs.

People often talk about a writer's voice. Quite early, I had a very physical sense of what it was. And the black singers I heard—Billie Holiday and Sarah Vaughan, and particularly Dinah Washington—had a lot of influence on my sense of the art of the voice, the voice's particular nuances.

So all this was brewing in me for a long time before I ever consciously wanted to write, but my problem always was to take that rich oral eloquence and try to do something with it. In making this transition, writers like Faulkner and Hardy and Ellison, all great storytellers, were very helpful to me.

I was drawn to the Bible as a connection, as a source. The Bible is an organic text in the life of blacks. The eloquence of the prophets in the Old Testament is recombined into a kind of literary resiliency.

In the Chicago of my youth, a wonderful range of Negro preaching was available. The art of the folk preacher has often provided my writing with a base. Aretha Franklin's father, C. L. Franklin, was one of America's tremendous preachers—his sermons were recorded, and I knew of them. They touched me with an oral, verbal immediacy, but also made some interesting stabs at an intellectual framework.

This is the thing: to move from that verbal emotion and ecstasy into a higher state of literary consciousness. The poems of Dylan Thomas and Yeats and particularly the sermons of John Donne brought occasions like marriage and death to a higher pitch, a more profound eloquence.

I'm Catholic on my mother's side. My mother's people are from Louisiana and my father's from Mississippi. It's through his family that I became aware of the gospel voice.

These two sides of my family—Mississippi on the one hand, Louisiana on the other—were both very much a part of the oral tradition and the oral education that I received.

What the writer learns outside of school is as important as what he or she learns inside it. I've always been overwhelmed by the bold blast of music out of Creole culture, the outrageousness of the New Orleans experience. It gave life to jazz, to honky-tonk, to cuisine. And it's produced some really outrageous and complex people, subtle with all kinds of shadings that have to do with the connections of French and Spanish and African character. The intergroup racism about color within that culture is heartbreaking, but at the same time, I greatly admired the energy of the culture. Together, New Orleans and Mississippi represented a kind of mythical Old Country for me, as the South did for James Baldwin. Baldwin didn't grow up in the South; he was a New Yorker.

All my cousins on my mother's side went to Catholic school at a time when Catholics did very little to encourage learning about the richness of black culture. I went to the Wendell Phillips grade school, an all-black public school in Chicago. I later went on to a predominantly white high school and college. Wendell Phillips was helpful in securing my identity. But I always went to a Catholic church, and there I was very much impressed with the ritual.

Interest in ritual and myth carried over into my writing. But I got a much better grounding in racial sensibility from the Protestant side and from some wonderful black teachers at Wendell Phillips.

In some ways, we benefited at Phillips because of the lack of opportunities available to our teachers. We had all these wonderful women, and a few men, too, who threw their lives into their teaching. They were what we used to call race men and women. They provided a certain racial uplift—within segregation, but they were always grounding us in the tradition of new writers: Paul Laurence Dunbar, Langston Hughes, Richard Wright.

Hyde Park High School, which I attended afterward, was predominantly white. In educational quality it ranked about fifteenth in the country and second or third in the state. It was a magnet for upper-middle-class Jewish families and for a few black families. A lot of students were the children of University of Chicago faculty. We had some extraordinary teachers there, all white, who had taught for thirty or forty years.

I was a Hyde Park from 1951 to 1955. By the time I graduated, about twothirds of the entering freshmen were black. So it was a time of transition. The transition from mostly white to mostly black happened very rapidly, and there was no attempt to do something for the average student or the mediocre student or the student who had little preparation. Meanwhile, a lot of the legendary teachers were either getting pretty old or had sort of lost interest. It was a wonderfully competitive environment, and it was great if you were competitive and ambitious, but otherwise you could get lost.

When I graduated, I went first of all to Woodrow Wilson Junior College, then to Roosevelt, and then to the University of Chicago. At the same time, my parents had divorced and my mother had remarried. She married a man who had a tavern, and I dropped out of college and started working there. Then I went into the army. When I came back, I re-enrolled at Chicago as a student at large. So I didn't take a degree, but I took a great many literature courses.

It's very important to the education of a writer that he or she find an intellectual mother or father. At Hyde Park High School, I had an extraordinary teacher, Mrs. Edith Thompson, who was interested in creative writing. I wanted to write poetry, and she was my mentor. She encouraged me; I became president of our creative writing class.

Then Mrs. Thompson was accused of running an abortion ring! Eventually the police rescinded this rap, and she was officially reinstated, but she never returned to teach. I went to the principal about it, and we students circulated a petition—but she didn't come back.

This brought out a couple of qualities in me that I hadn't known about. One was that I could become a fighter when somebody was mistreated. (When the crisis in Mrs. Thompson's life came along, I saw it as an attack on a mother figure.) Another was loyalty.

Later, Allison Davis was an intellectual father to me. He was a cultural anthropologist who taught in the University of Chicago's School of Education. His specialties were the gifted child and educational psychology. Davis was the first black to get tenure at a major Northern university. I met him at International House about 1966, and we struck up a friendship that lasted many years. My first novel was dedicated to Allison. He had a strong influence on my thinking and writing. Though he was a scholar and not a novelist, he had broad literary interests that made him a valued intellectual colleague.

Another influence on my intellectual growth was a University of Chicago professor named Perrin Lowrey was an authority on Faulkner. He was also a writer and had published a collection of short stories. He was a Southerner, a Mississippian. I took creative writing classes with him.

Lowrey was an intellectual uncle to me. He introduced me to certain books and also to the idea that the writer must develop a critical intelligence.

Previously, my writing had mainly been drawn from spiritual and emotional juices.

Through Lowrey I met a junior colleague of his, John Cawelti. Cawelti and I struck up an acquaintanceship that has flowered over the years. (In fact, Cawelti wrote the introduction to one of my recently reissued novels.) Another professor who influenced me was Marvin Mirsky, with whom I took many classes. Mirsky was one of the finest teachers I ever had—vastly well read, wonderfully analytical about literature.

I took a creative writing class from John Logan—a wonderful poet who had an extraordinary life. Naomi Lazard was one of the poets in the class, and others came out of it too.

I met Marge Piercy through a writing group that me in Hyde Park. There were about thirty people in the group—all white except one or two; we would meet twice a month. I sort of floated in and out.

At the time, Piercy was writing poetry, not fiction. Of all of us, she had the best intellect. She was a good critic, intelligent, very well read. And she was involved with a friend of mine, a Southerner who was a writer. Like many others in the group, he was very talented but never published anything. This fellow even had a contract for a novel but never finished it. Subsequently, he drifted away. We also had a Trinidadian writer who was so talented, a wonderful storyteller. He had a large family back in Trinidad, and he got caught up in real estate. Another writer in the group, who published many novels, was Harry Mark Petrakis. I remember I was in class when Petrakis sold his first short story. He had been writing for years.

Figures like these are important in the life of a writer. They encourage you in times of crisis in your own life—crises in confidence or times when you are fumbling with this yeast of talent to convert it into something else. If intellectual fathering or mothering is going to work well, it must happen in a natural, uncalculated way. I stumbled into Mrs. Thompson—and certainly into Allison.

A writer needs three educations: to read a great deal; to listen a lot (that's oral tradition); and to learn the actual craft of writing, which comes through imitating very good writers. You're usually drawn to your own writing by being overwhelmed or fascinated by some other writer. Of course, you break away from imitation through rewriting and through the assertion of your will, your ego, your style, and your own material. To make such breakthroughs requires the kind of intellectual ability that is nurtured by a university.

To be a writer of substance, you have to be something of an intellectual, though not necessarily a scholar—hopefully not! Oh dear, sitting around, hovering over one play by Shakespeare all my life? No, not that. But there must be intellectual fire. Some of that was always there, for me, yet it was only smoldering, almost smothered by an avalanche of literary influences.

I've always been very much taken with the possibility of capturing a sensibility through language and transforming oral eloquence into literary eloquence. The writers who most influenced me were writers who were in the first instance poets. Thomas Hardy was one of the first, along with Edgar Allan Poe, and then in college Faulkner and James Joyce. Another was Dylan Thomas. For a long time, I also wanted to write plays, and felt attracted to certain writers—Eugene O'Neill and Tennessee Williams among them—who were poets of the theater. These writers overwhelmed me with the poetry of their art.

In the early seventies, I began to get interested in Russian literature. It was a real source. At the same time, I became quite interested in Latin American literature. The Latin American writers were wrestling with some of the same problems I was: how to take an essentially oral culture and transform it into a literary one; how to deal with the problem of slavery, the problem of belonging to an oppressed people. The bold and outrageous literature of Garcia Marquez and Jose Donoso gave me boldness.

The black writers whom I admired, too—Robert Hayden and Ellison—were interested in much the same transformation. *Invisible Man* impressed me. It was Ellison's eloquence, and his great storytelling, that did it. These were the things I really hungered for in my fiction.

I had great problems with the black aesthetic, and shunned it. I saw the Black Arts movement as a dead end. For that reason, I didn't have a lot of contact with black writers—with the black young writers who were part of that movement.

I thought it was a segregationist movement, limited and limiting. I thought that it was racist and that it short-circuited the great richness of black life. I was very attracted to certain dimensions of race pride, but the movement was intellectually dead.

The Irish writers I most admired had handled nationalism with such cunning and depth. You need some of this; it's part of the rise of any people. But the narrowness of nationalism can cut you off from developing intellectually. You can get caught up in the worship of your culture to a point where it is parochial and pretentious. It can keep you from taking on the viable connections to world culture. It can keep you from being critical of you own culture. You need some of that nationalistic energy to foster a political movement and a culture movement. But if you don't take that to the next step, which is a broadness and a flowering, it can be deadly. That's what I saw happening with the black aesthetic movement.

During my days as a University of Chicago student, a lot of black writers were trying to make art out of polemics, instead of transforming the polemics of the culture into art. I was working as a newspaperman while I was a student, and this gave me a way to deal directly with the visceral political issues of the day. That was very healthy, because it forced me, when I came home to write fiction, to try something else. When I came to my own fiction, I could work in the way of an artist, which is what I'd always wanted to do. I thought that this could be the most meaningful and moving contribution to my people and to myself—to develop my talent into an instrument that was artful and angular and layered and transformed. Multilayered. As complicated as African Americans are. Irreducible.

Malcolm X to me represented this kind of angularity of character, what Dostoyevsky calls a soul struggle in terms of politics and religion: he was constantly, passionately in search of who he was. Whereas a lot of my polemical friends were bowled over by Malcolm as knowing who he was, I saw the man as divided, in chaos.

All these writers educated me and gave me confidence in using and shaping certain materials in my own culture. But when you're overwhelmed by someone or something, you do have to step back at some point. That's very true. It's true in love. And I felt that way, certainly, with these writers and also with the great black entertainers who made such an impression on me: Mahalia Jackson, the great dancers, the wonderful singers, the tap dancers. All of them were overwhelming figures. So I've always had to try to move back from all that, to pick myself up.

How do I pick myself up? Well, it takes a long time to do it. Ultimately, of course, it's the life of the mind that makes you do it. One of the things I had to ferret out was how and why I was ultimately drawn to these people. You're drawn because you're nourished by these personalities; the meaning of life is revealed. But in the initial stages—the stages you pass through when you are young—it's the emotional fire that counts. And you may not understand, at first. Your need is too great.

As a young man, I was chaotic and romantic, like my father. I was always falling in and out of love, being overwhelmed by female beauty, and so on. And in a way, that's necessary. It's necessary that life overwhelm you, and you engage, and then out of that try to shape something. It's struggle that's good.

Yet the older I've grown, the more fascinated I've become with the artists who've lived long lives. Maybe they have more wisdom. Maybe they have stepped back. The life of the mind—and a spiritual life—has had time to flower and flourish.

I'm less romantic now. I'm attracted to a certain lyricism and fire and magic, but, conversely, it's hard to achieve that and a certain kind of maturation, too. Romanticism must give way to other things, such as spiritual development. A certain combativeness is part of the romantic identity, a kind of foolishness in seeking perfection in love and in yourself and in others. When you are so devouring of other people, you don't allow them to flower, or yourself.

Obviously, as art takes over your life, you have to be more and more a kind of priest and live with your own solitude. To find that state of mind is very difficult. When you find it, you have to accept the fact that you're married to your art.

Though I'm less romantic now, I still love the romance of life. It's a very difficult thing to maintain, because of the crassness of the world. A lot of people take romance to the point of a kind of corruption of feeling. The life of an academic constantly show up the absurdity in this.

The University of Chicago was, and still is, a place of high intellect and high art, and a place where one learns to appreciate one's solitude. It's all right to be a priest of solitude there.

# "Beyond the Hard Work and Discipline": An Interview with Leon Forrest

Charles H. Rowell / 1997

From *Callaloo* 20:2 (1997), 342–56. © Charles H. Rowell. Reprinted with permission of The Johns Hopkins University Press.

**Rowell:** In the opening to your nonfiction prose piece in *Swing Low: Black Men Writing* (ed. Rebecca Carroll), you make the following statement: "Beyond the hard work and discipline, no one knows what makes the magic of writing." "Magic," "hardwork" and "discipline"—these words keep echoing in my head. Will you say more about magic, hardwork and discipline as they relate to the craft of writing?

**Forrest:** Well, I had originally wanted to be a poet. It seems to me that it's in the poetry of language, what we call the prose style, and also finding the poetry of an individual character in his or her personality that brings on this sense of uniqueness. And I suppose that in the subterranean regions of my own psyche, let's say, I've wanted to create a poem on each page of my prose, and if I can do that then I'm close to this magic. The magic is the ability to transform the reader's imagination into something other and strange as he or she is confronting my text. How often that works? I don't know. It probably doesn't work nearly as much as I'd like it to, but the books that I read, the novels that I most admire, are novels in which there is a high degree of poetic sensibility that is part of the magic of making the text something else, something enduring—something possessing within it a constant resonance every time you return to the novel. You might read a great novel like *The Sound and the Fury* or *Invisible Man* every three or four years, but each time there is something marvelous and new and magical about it.

**Rowell:** What do you mean when you say "the poetic" in reference to prose fiction? I have my own ideas of what poetic prose is—that is, lyrical phrasings, musically, etc. Of course, I am not saying all; there is much more. I am certain you meant much more.

**Forrest:** Well, yes. But you're saying a lot. I agree that that's the first condition of it. Then that lyricism—that's a good word for it really—is emotional. That's the first thing. It must be that. And then spiritual and, finally, very intellectual. Well, we're attracted to it because of the emotional ring of beauty and also the fire of it. So that's another condition I would say, a certain fire to it. And I seem to be most attracted to the novelists who are poets. I hadn't thought about that until recently. Thomas Hardy, the great English writer, was the first novelist I read seriously, and I still read him. He certainly was poet of the novel. And I would say Faulkner and certainly Ellison. There's a high degree of this in Toni Morrison. I was just mentioning it about John Edgar Wideman. And I don't know Spanish at all, but I certainly get the sense of this Great poetic power to transform in Gabriel García Márquez—another writer who has influenced me a lot. So I'm drawn to this. Now the problem though, going from poet to novelist, is that I had to say, well finally, that I am a novelist; I am interested in character and so on, so that's where I have to plum the depths of human personality. But even there the lyricism, the particular lyricism of a character, is important to me. Lyricism can refer to an attribute of someone's character and the way they voice things, the way they articulate their problems or their strengths in a most succinct way.

I was teaching *Song of Solomon* the other day, and I was talking about a particular character in the novel—the character Ruth, who is very objectionable in a lot of ways, and yet Morrison has this capacity to reach into the pits of her characters and find there the poetry within their souls. There are one or two very good monologues of Ruth that really turn into soliloquies. They're simple and so on, but they have the ring of the particular character of her soul—that is, of Ruth's soul. So I have a broad definition for poetry.

Now the other thing though, as you are aware, is that I was raised on listening to the great singers, the great African-American singers—Billie Holiday, Sarah Vaughn, Nat King Cole, Dinah Washington, Billy Eckstine—I could go on and on. And then the great white singers as well, like Frank Sinatra and other wonderful Italian singers. That introduced within my consciousness a sense of the poetry in language and song, and voicing this poetry. No one would ever confuse Sarah Vaughn with Billie Holiday, for instance, or Dinah Washington with Ella Fitzgerald. So it was very much etched in my consciousness as a young child, the poetry of these great singers. Many of them were female. As you know, I have a particular interest in female characters in my novels. Well, this is all related to the question you raised about possibilities of poetic expression.

**Rowell:** I think you said that you were first a poet and later became a novelist. The range of the poet, the landscape of the poet, seems much more confined than that of the novelist—unless he or she is writing the narrative poem like *Paradise Lost, Omeros* or *The Prelude*, for example. The range in these is not the range we generally find in poems. That is, the poem has certain linguistic, as well as particular formal, controls. The novel, too, has its own formal demands. While the poet suggests much in concentrated language, the novelist can show us big landscapes, sustained periods of time, characters developing, etc. How did you negotiate the crossing over from the poet to the novelist, from one aesthetic sensibility to another?

**Forrest:** Well, that's beautifully expressed the way put it. I guess maybe the movement from each of my novels has really been a progression of that sort, and something I've gained—I wasn't terribly conscious of it. The most poetic of my novels would be the first one, *There Is a Tree More Ancient than Eden*—there I was trying to work with poetry in, really, the epic form. And the epic form then moves us into the next stage in creative form, and that would be the novel. Though I don't rate the novel over the epic, for goodness' sake; nor do I rate the novel over poetry. But that seems to be the progression historically. And that seems to be my progression—what with the rise of the novel in the 18th and particularly the 19th century in Europe and Russia, with the rise certainly of the bourgeoisie and the interest in family life, and so on. All those became more and more my concern. So you can move right along from *The Bloodworth Orphans* to *Two Wings to Veil My Face* and, then, *Divine Days*, which is very much centered in story and character and jokes and questions of morality and characterization. So I have probably moved away from poetry—but it was a slow progression, because I published *There Is a Tree More Ancient than Eden* in 1973, and I didn't publish *Divine Days* until 1992. That's almost a twenty year span of my career, but it is a movement, I think, from a high degree of concentration in the poetic to more and more the demands of the novel. You're absolutely right: there are these rich and formal demands of the novel—no matter how much many of the people I most admire have broken the form and remade the form again, like Joyce and Faulkner.

**Rowell:** I want to argue with you about the European novel, but I will not. You said that the European novel evolved as narrative form moved from the epic to the novel. I want to argue that the European novel as narrative moved from the epic to the romance to the novel. But let's not focus on the European origins of the novel; let's focus on the novel as form evolving in the American context. The American novel—The American Novel—built upon that European form, but the American novel is strongly influenced by our 19th-century vernacular traditions—storytelling, for example.

**Forrest:** Yes. That's right. That's right. Yes. You're absolutely right. That's a great thing with Twain and Faulkner and Ellison and Chestnutt to some degree. So you're right about that. And I—even from the beginning, even with *There Is a Tree*—was very much interested in the idiomatic or the vernacular and as all a part of the landscape. Actually there is an attempt at a fairly broad landscape for all of the narrowness plot-wise in *There Is a Tree*. But each novel placed a different intellectual demand on me. As I said, in *There Is a Tree* I wanted really to create a kind of epic poem as novel, I would say. Then with *The Bloodworth Orphans* there was so much criticism: "Well you Know, *There Is a Tree* is very interesting. The language is, you know, marvelous," some People said, "but where are the characters?" Well, there were character sketches in there but not character development as such, so my obsession with *The Bloodworth Orphans* was to write novel which was just chock full of characters, which it is. And also it was a novel that you could pretty much define easily, at least in the sense of saying that this is a novel about a lot of characters and the major ones are orphans. So then with *Two Wings*, I wanted to concentrate on the life of one particular person and go back into the heritage of slavery and so on. Then, you know, with *Divine Days*, I was after the broadest kind of landscape, at least that I could conceive of, with all these voices; and I really wanted to see, as always, how much of the texture of jazz and that poetry could get in there. Jazz could be a way of ordering the structure of the novel, I thought, and to some degree I've tried it. I don't know how much I've succeeded. And then also I was very much under the influence too, as I guess all contemporary writers are, of the way in which Joyce cracked open the novel form in *Ulysses*. So those were just some of the things involved. But here again, Joyce is so interested in capturing the vernacular of Irish speech and peasant speech. So all these things work together in some strange brewing way within the unconscious, subterranean process.

The other thing that I should say, too, Charles, is that for me writing is endless rewriting, over and over again. That goes back to my interests in reading poetry. One of the poets who had such a huge influence on me was Dylan Thomas, and when I was around my late teens, early twenties, I really fell in love with so many of his major poems. And then I discovered that what seemed to me to be the great ease of literary eloquence in his writing was often the result of about two hundred revisions. Every time he would make a change—one small change even—he'd copy the poem all over again in long hand in order to see the growth of the poem. So when I discovered this, I said, "Well, I don't think I have the fortitude to become a poet." [*Laughter.*] But the point is that writing demands the most acute kind of self discipline, and it's so private in that sense. You know that as well, and it's hard to convey that to young people. All they see is the finished product. They don't realize the scores of rehearsals that went into this wonderful dance act.

**Rowell:** Will you amplify that metaphor, that the young writer does not "realize the scores of rehearsals that went into this dance act"?
**Forrest:** Yes. It's a little bit like our going to a wonderful play or to a performance by the Alvin Ailey Dancers, a great dance team, and there seems to be a marvelous aesthetic in their performance—a blend of rhythm, intelligence, spirituality, set to such a high pitch that it seems to be almost perfection in itself. That's all we see. But if we were journalists and had to cover them for the press, and we had to go there and see them in all their rehearsals again and again, we'd probably say, "My, I couldn't take this." But that's exactly what's necessary to bring them to that high pitch of excellence—these rehearsals. They must rehearse scores of times to get a particular routine to perfection. So that's what we see on that particular night when we go to watch them perform. Well, the writer is involved in the same thing with his or her rewrites—for me anyway.

Many writers don't need to rewrite as much as I seem to need that. Rewriting gives me inspiration. I'll put something away for a long time and then come back to it, and start writing or just typing it actually, honestly, and then suddenly something will flash and then, oh, this needs something else. This suggests something else. Of course putting a piece of writing aside is very important for me because I can come back to it with a certain toughness, a certain editor-like anger. Anger, outrage, aggression—all of these are

very important forces that the writer or the artist needs to redirect into his
writing, to push him or her along.

**Rowell:** I want to go back to what you were speaking of as the poetic in prose
fiction. Immediately think of the lyricism of William Faulkner's *Absalom,
Absalom!* and Ralph Ellison's *Invisible Man*—for example, the opening with
Rosa Coldfield summoning Quentin Compson to her home in Mississippi,
and then Rev. Homer Barbee's sermon at the black college in the deepest
South. Those are wonderful passages. Let's not forget that beautiful poetry
in Toni Morrison's *Sula*. Then there is also the poetry of your own fiction.
Is there a passage in your own fiction which, for its lyricism or whatever,
satisfies—or almost satisfies—you?

**Forrest:** You're right there: these passages you cite are moments of perfection. I would say Quentin's monologue too. I think that's such a good question to raise because the point is that the writer is measuring him- or herself
against these moments of great perfection in other writers, like the opening
of *Absalom, Absalom!* One of the great achievements about that is Faulkner's
ability to sustain Rosa Coldfield's voice. It's so clear and, amid its complexity,
you know that that's her voice. And that's really Rev. Barbee's voice is *Invisible
Man*—that long marvelous monologue. I don't know that I've ever achieved
that. I mean that would be something for a critic to see or not to see. I may
perhaps have come close to it in some of the preachers in my novels. But,
again, that's even dangerous for a writer to say, because if I thought I had
achieved some perfection in something, I might not try to write anymore.
I might say, well, why go on and do this? So it's really, I think, the insecurity
of the writer that often drives us—that I can't do this, but I will as sure as hell
try. And out of that tension a writer may create something new. But if I come
to the typewriter too cocky about my characters, then I'll never do anything.
I've got to have a lot of confidence—which I think I do—that I can write, but
I also have this concomitant insecurity that I won't be able to achieve that
which I have set before me. Because I've set before me—and I don't think this
is too bold for me to say—usually so large a task in my novels: I try to mea-
sure up to those tasks, but I don't think I ever have. Obviously, this was the
great drive in *Divine Days*. But I have no way of knowing how much of that
novel succeeds. I think some of it does, but it'll take years and years of critics
and people who have read it to say, well, this is stronger than this, this works
better than this. I don't know—but my ambition was there, and the writers

I most admire are writers with a large ambition. And then when I read them, I say, oh, I want to do that too. I want to see if I can outdo that. I like that with Toni a lot. I like that with Wideman a lot. They have large ambitions. Without a large ambition, why write, for heaven's sake? Why not just do something else?

**Rowell:** I think I want to ask that same question another way. Is there a passage or scene in your work that gives you great pleasure when you go back to read it? If so, will you explain why?

**Forrest:** I guess one of the novels that's closest to me is *The Bloodworth Orphans*, because it's the one that always has the least appreciation, and people always have trouble with it more than any of my other novels. But there's a scene in there, oh I don't know, maybe around page 70 and so, that I often read when I give readings. It's a little monologue about four pages long of a religious woman who's really a religious fanatic—she's a blind prophetess, Rachel Flowers, and she's talking about her past and this garment that she's found in the South that she takes up and uses in so many different ways. It's about for pages, and I always find myself coming back to it to read in public places. So it may be that that's one of my favorite scenes. Often too there'll be some other scene that I like to read and read aloud, and I'll say, "oh, why didn't I cut that out?" or "why didn't I add to that?" But ultimately what I might like best in my writing might not be that which is the most successful. And therefore the role of the critic—the role, really, of the generations to come along— is to say these things. You know, it's like if you have children, I suppose, and people are pointing these things out to you about your children. You know your children in a general way and an intimate way, but maybe their teachers or lovers or friends may see certain things about them to you've missed. So that's what I would have to say about my work. And again, to emphasize the importance of the tension between insecurity, on the one hand, and a sense, on the other, of "Look, I can do anything at the typewriter." And the writer goes back and forth—or this writer does anyway—between these two psychic worlds, vacillates between them.

**Rowell:** What is the "insecurity" you refer to?

**Forrest:** Well, you're measuring yourself against the best that's gone, in your own particular genre. Apparently you've come to writing, in my case, because this was all that I could do I was never . . . I was a good student in class, but never a great student. In public speaking I was sort of average. I was always interested in public speaking and language, but there were always people who could out-talk me in the barbershop, in the bar, talking to the girls. There was always someone who could talk rings around me. But I knew when I would go home and try to write things—my little poems, or essays, or sketches I was doing—that that was something that had a uniqueness to it, and early on teachers saw that. But in the larger African American arena, particularly in a culture that places such emphasis on oral tradition, I was always in the background. I was always way in the middle group. So, that was always a propelling force with me juxtaposed with the fact that I could write, and it was obvious that I had some talent—didn't know, and still don't, how much—but it was only there before the typewriter or with my little pad that I could begin to develop some of these sketches. So the insecurity is important, and I don't think I've ever lost that. I don't go to the idea about . . . what is that, anguish of tradition? anxiety of influence?—I don't go to that at all. But when I read these great writers—and you raised a good question—here's a sentence in Ellison or Morrison or here's a characterization in Dostoyevsky no one will ever match or that Leon Forrest will never match. And I bow to that, and yet I turn around ten minutes later and say, "Hell, I'm going to see if I can't match it." You see the duality there? [*Laughter.*] And so it goes. Those are some of the sources of insecurities.

I was even thinking this about John Edgar Wideman the other night. He gave such a beautiful statement about my work, and I was saying, "My goodness, I could never do that just off the cuff." I could do it maybe, if you gave me a couple of days to work on it. But I couldn't do it just with that spontaneity, and I admire it a great deal. My friend Jan Carew has that—I know you must know his work—just as a speaker, and Ralph Ellison had it. Ralph had a marvelous ability to speak with such eloquence on the spot on anything, or tell a story on anything and just be marvelous. So I greatly admire that and greatly desire to do that, but the place I've found that I can do it best is at the typewriter.

**Rowell:** Will you relate the circumstances surrounding your becoming a novelist? In your other *Callaloo* interview with Kenneth Warren, you talk about the influence of the storytelling tradition.

**Forrest:** That was part of an insecurity by the way, and the overwhelming thing, because you know I am sixty years old and I came along at a time when, you know, I was the only child of two only children. All the adults around me were telling stories and so on. And you just didn't enter their dialogue. You just sat there and listened. You wouldn't dare open your mouth. So that created a fascination with storytelling, on the one hand, and then with how to transform that into literature later on. On the other hand, it was intimidating. I said, "My god, here's uncle so and so who can tell these great stories and all these marvelous liars in my family and I can't do that, even now." But what I can do is this: if you give me a nugget of a story, something has happened to you, and I might take that and develop it and blow on it, like you might blow on a flame, and set that to something that might surprise you. But I can't do that on an immediate extemporaneous basis. So that was another benefit I had in being surrounded by these storytellers and, at the same time, a form of intimidation.

Where did I find out the poetic power or the power to write? Well, there are a lot of benefits, there again, in being an only child. An only child to only children, I had my own room. My teachers say some of this in me early. I came from a family of people who would encourage you to do things. They certainly worried about me writing. I had a wonderful black teacher at one of the grade schools who took an interest in me. I had good teachers at an integrated school in Hyde Park that saw a talent in me when I was in high school. But, as you know, literary talent is the last to develop, so I had to learn what other writers did about developing their talents. Again, the options available to me at the time weren't that many. Baldwin was just publishing, and Ellison had published *Invisible Man* when I was fifteen, but I didn't read that until I was maybe almost in college. I did go to a wonderful black grade school where we read Langston Hughes, Countee Cullen, and Richard Wright. We were aware of W. E. B. Du Bois. So that was a great benefit. I did have a sense of a tradition that influenced me—Sterling Brown. But I had to find out what a writer needs to do, and how he has to live a certain way and develop the imagination. That's one thing: developing a writer's kind of memory. I don't say that my memory is better than anyone else's. In fact, it's probably just very mediocre. But what I have is an ability to file things away that can be significant to what I need. Developing a highly associative intelligence is very important to a writer. So I see something that reminds me of something else, either something I've read or something I've worked on, and I'm storing all of this away in a private vault to be called out who knows when.

**Rowell:** You said that you had to learn what a writer had to do. How did you learn that?

**Forrest:** Well, by learning to read texts in a critical way that I had fallen in love with in an emotional way. That was true with the great peoms of Dylan Thomas, and that was true of Ellison, Baldwin, Faulkner, Thomas Hardy, who are all, as you think about it, writers who have a wonderful kind of emotional energy to their work. But then I had to go back and learn to read them critically. So I developed a critical intelligence, and the next step after that was to develop a sense of how these writers were doing some of these things in terms of making a connection to the reader's imagination. So later on I was saying, "Ah, now I see what he's doing technically about this." You know, I was talking about Quentin's monologue—it becomes a soliloquy in some ways—in *The Sound and the Fury*. Well, there are all kinds of techniques available going on there for the writer. And that goes beyond what the literary critic might see. That is to say that I'm reading this monologue in all kinds of ways to find out what I can learn from Faulkner technically. Or in Barbee's monologue I am learning to see how Ellison was able to transfrom the oral tradition into the literary tradition in that monologue. And that's going to be very helpful to me as I develop as a writer. I didn't want to be another writer who just recreated what was on a tape recorder of a sermon. I had to make those sermons literary sermons. And that's the thing I admire in Ellison. I certainly admire it again in *Moby Dick*, and to some degree the preacher, Shegog, in *The Sound and the Fury*, and all those instances when these writers evoke the folk preachers. Of course, as we know, the folk preacher is central to understanding the culture. I used to listen to a lot of C. L. Franklin's sermons on tape, over and over again. He was very important to me. Then the next thing I had to do was say, "Look, I can't be a preacher. I have no desire to be a preacher, but I know if I'm going to be a writer, an African American writer, I've got to deal with that black preacher; and to some degree, no one has dealt with it the way I want to." So I've got to say, "I love Ellison because I knew him personally and loved his book, and was very much influenced by Faulkner; but I've got to beat those guys. I've got to go beyond them. And here's an avenue to do it." No one has really done very much, when you think about it, with the art of the folk preacher in our novels or one the stage. So I said, "ah, here's a chance to make my way," and of course it fit wonderfully well for me because I wanted to find avenues into the culture that had not been explored very much by other black writers. Finding that art and trying to develop it has been very dear to me, and it haunts all of my novels. It also was very useful too because, as you know, I am more interested in the issues of the religious experience, spiritual experience, probably than any other of my black contemporaries.

**Rowell:** Did you say spiritual or religious?
**Forrest:** Spiritual and religious.

**Rowell:** Will you, as a writer, speak, just for a moment, on the difference between the spiritual and the religious?
**Forrest:** Sure. You may have characters—and we know people like this—who have a wonderful cluster of spirituality and cultural energy. That would be true with someone like Pilot, for instance, in *Song of Solomon*. Yet she wouldn't be religious in the way we speak of it in terms of Christ and the Judeo-Christian heritage. We don't know of her going to any particular churches, and we'd be surprised if she did. Yet she certainly is a spiritual person. Later on in *Beloved* there is a marvelous character, Baby Suggs, who goes from church to church, and finally evokes a kind of sermon that is African as much as anything. Well, I'm much more interested in the Judeo-Christian heritage in a traditional way and my characters, you know, are pretty much bound in those traditions, and amid that there are Catholics, there are Baptists, there are some Muslims too in my novels. In fact I've known many Marxists who were some of the most spiritual people that you could find in terms of wanting to change the world and do good things. If you mention going to church, they're ready to shoot you. [*Laughter.*] And we've known two people who were very religious who didn't have much of a soul. [*Laughter.*]

**Rowell:** Will you talk about the differences in reading as a creative writer and reading as a critic or general reader? How do these practices differ?
**Forrest:** I guess it comes back to something corny in a certain way, because I still talk about being in love with certain novels of Thomas Hardy, or certain things that I reread all the time in *Anna Karenina*, or some things I'll reread again and again in Ellison. I'm really looking for the magic there. In that sense, my connection is to the average but good, solid reader. As you know, you dare not mention around academic circles that you love this book or you love this passage. People would think you're crazy, because they assume that love means that your critical intelligence is being limited. But I'm interested in consuming everything I can get my hands on in a rich passage and coming

back to it and getting new energies from it. I guess that's the thing. I'm always looking for new energies for my own writing, and it may be that I'll get this from reading something, rereading something wonderful, out of a passage in a novel or a play or a poem that I haven't read in a long time. There is a certain lightning there. There is a certain energizing magic there. I think you can abuse it by reading it too much or too often. You need to leave these things alone and come back to them. That's just like some great particular cuisine that you like, but you don't want to have this particular dinner every week—even though you'd like to—maybe once a month or something. So it maintains a wonderment for you. I'm looking for that wonderment always in other writers, and then I'm seeing if I can get a spark from that to energize my own work. Writers in that sense are certainly thieves. Take anything to energize yourself. I don't have any problems with that at all, because that's how you promote the literature. I have heard these folk preachers. I saw what Ellison did with them and saw what Faulkner did with them. Now I'm going to try to do something else, something different and better. You always should want to do something better than the writers you admire.

I was telling a colleague of mine once that the greatest tribute I could give to Ralph Ellison would be to write a better novel than *Invisible Man*, and this person was so shocked to hear me say that. Well, I'm sure Ralph would very much appreciate that. You know, with our students, we want them to go beyond us, for heaven's sake. How's the world going to improve if they don't? So I don't have any problems about that. These are standards that these writers have set out there before us to match. It's probably kind of macho, I suppose. My father and my uncles were always taking me around to boxing matches—and I've been a great fan of boxing all of my life—and there was always this idea of out-boxing whoever was the best. And of course there was an old saying or question in the barbershop, "Was Ali better than Joe Louis?" Or "Could Ray Robinson beat this fighter?" And these were very dear things and deep in the culture. It's still there, but now transformed of course to football and basketball. But that's part of my matrix, my ethos, so I bring that to my writing—that sense of wanting to out-box my competitors. Not my contemporaries, particularly, but all those people up there on the shelf—see if I can get me some shelf space. [*Laughter*.]

**Rowell:** What would you say if I told you that the barbershop for me is a vernacular university with an invisible library?

**Forrest:** That's a great statement. Sure. I couldn't agree with you more. Yes. Oh, yes. That's right. Even now when I come in: "Oh, here's Professor Forrest." But even now, I'm quiet in there because there are so many of these voices, so much intelligence, so much lying that goes on in there. The barber told me the other week, he said "You know what I want you to do? I want you to help me do a book, Forrest, because you know there's so much bullshit out here and lying." I almost fell out. I said, "Matt, don't you ever contemplate cutting off the lying going on in this barbershop." In these exaggerations we come closer, of course, to something that's greater than any attempt to pinpoint truth—all these stories and fables and so on. And out of that you develop something. No, I couldn't agree with you more. And I would say that my newspaper work too has perhaps been a better training for me than even university life. As you know, I don't have a degree. Oh, I took all kinds of courses from three universities and so on, but I have found my training as a journalist, making these deadlines—I've got to write three or four pages in a day—I've got a deadline and I'm doing something on a book review. All of these things were helpful to me. I should say that my background as a journalist was very helpful to me in toughening me up in having editors look at my copy and say, "This is horrible," and throw it in the wastebasket. All of that is toughening to the writer. The writer needs this. Set deadlines for yourself. I want to have this accomplished by the end of the summer . . .

It's a tradition that supported me for about ten years, and I've tried to keep it alive, since I've been working here at Northwestern University, by doing regular book reviews and essays. I felt this the other night when they made a tribute to me at the Chicago Art Institute—to keep alive the continuities of my life, whether it be friendships, or my teaching—I'm in my 24th year here—or developing a sustained body of work. All these continuities are very important to me just in a personal way, but also in a way that's the relationship of the artist to his life, because we live in a country that is so damn brittle, a country in which it is so hard to develop and maintain continuities and patterns. People are moving all over, changing directions in their careers; relatives that you knew as a child moved to another part of the country, and you can't get in touch with them, you don't see them. By the way, that's one of the great things about the barbershop. I'll go in there, and there will be people who have been coming in there for thirty years. And there are bars where I'll go, and there are people who have been going to his bar, drinking in these bars since the early 1960s. So that gives me a continuity and a pattern, and the novel is very much involved with finding these continuities in society amid the chaos and amid the tremendous changes within the personality of American society.

**Rowell:** You began your writing career when the literary establishment and the academy publicly denigrated African American literature and the African American author. There were no journals devoted exclusively, for example, to creative writing by African Americans. Of course, there was *Negro Digest*, which later became *Black World*. But that small general monthly could not sustain the whole of African American writers, especially fiction writers. Were there creative writing classes at universities in Chicago where you lived? Where did you find critical encouragement and support? Did you have anything to do with the Chicago South Side Arts Center? Please talk about your beginnings as a writer. Will you describe the apprenticeship for your writing career?

**Forrest:** Well, my apprenticeship had two parts. One would be my working in a bar; I was getting voices there all the time. Then I was taking classes at the University of Chicago when I returned from the army in 1962; I was taking creative literature courses and creative writing. I also was involved in a writers' group in Hyde Park, which was integrated though mainly white. Two well-known writers were in that group too. One would be Harry Mark Patraikas. I don't know if you know his work; he's a Greek writer in Chicago. And then there was Marge Piercy, the poet and novelist. It was a pretty good group. So I would bounce around between these three worlds, maybe four worlds, and out of that I was getting something quite nourishing. The other thing that was important: I was buddies with a lot of people in the arts, some jazz musicians, some actors, and so on. All of that was nourishing in this memory bank that I was developing and evolving—not in a particularly conscious way—but it was all put in there. And right along with coming in everyday and trying to write at the typewriter. The writer needs all of that going on, I would say, in his life, her life. And it's good if you can do that when you're quite young.

   As far as encouragement goes—I mentioned this too in one of the early essays in *The Furious Voice for Freedom*—I had a white professor at the University of Chicago, a Southerner who was quite an authority on Faulkner. He was a short story writer himself. His name was Perrin Lowrey, and he had published a volume of short stories and taught creative writing. He was a big influence on me. He also knew Ellison. He had been a good friend to Ellison, when Ralph taught at the University of Chicago between 1960 and 1961. He was there for a year. Lowrey had played jazz, and I think being a liberated white Southerner was nifty too, because he had an appreciation for black life that you don't normally see with white Yankees. So he was a wonderful influence. He was one of the first people to encourage me. He was aware of some of the wonderful Negro preaching they used to hear on the radio at times. And he was saying, "Well, I wonder if anybody is recording this, because this is some wonderful stuff." Anyway, he was a big influence. It was through him I met Cawelti, by the way. He was a senior to Cawelti, and so that developed a long friendship with Cawelti for thirty-five years.

Around this time, too—during the late 1960s—there was the development, the evolution of the Black Arts Movement which argued for the Black Aesthetic. Well, with my background—and you've read my novels—it just seemed to me to be the way I didn't want to go. But on the other hand, it had such currency in Chicago and throughout the country, the big cities. It kind of threw me for a loop. It seemed segregationist to me. Most of the people I knew who were writing, were writing poetry, and the poetry wasn't very good. A lot of it showed much energy, and that's certainly true with the Black Aesthetic. All my training—and I haven't changed from this at all—was integrative, not necessarily integration with white people, but integrative in the sense that I wanted to read the broadest library. It was—and is—open to me. And then I want to take these techniques back to the story of my people. That didn't seem to me to be evil. That didn't seem to me to be a sellout of the race. I mean if I was a black surgeon, and I told you that I only had studied diseases affecting black people, you would say, "That's fine Forrest, but what else do you know, because I've got to bring my aunt in here for surgery?" So that was my position. I wasn't as forward with it as I am now, but that was my general position. So I didn't have a lot of connection with some of the Chicago Black Aesthetic people. On the other hand, the people I began to admire came out of that, like Sterling Plumpp, for instance, and a few others. I think they got the best of it, got the energy and then reconnected it, in Sterling's case, to his Southern heritage and also the blues. So I had a double whammy there, in other words; I had difficulty—it was virtually impossible—getting published in the white magazines, and then of course the other thing was the difficulty dealing with the Black Aesthetic. And I may be absolutely wrong about this—this is just my read on it—in terms of what

wasn't working for me in it. There have been people who have emerged out
of it and have done quite well. More power to them, but it was just my read
on it for me. And then the two most influential black writers of the day, that
I thought so much of, were James Baldwin and Ralph Ellison. Well, they were
as removed from the Black Aesthetic as they could be. Baldwin was a big
influence on me in a time too, an influence in terms of those essays—the fire
of those essays and the language and intelligence. I read him as closely as
I did Ellison. Certainly he was very useful to me in terms of the religious
themes that he develops so beautifully in *Go Tell It on the Mountain.* Just the
fire of language and the poetry of it was really amazing. If anybody asked me
about that, I said, "Well, what about Ellison, what about Baldwin?" Again, my
insecurity and lostness and worry about where I fit into all this—issues of
identity, my own family riddled, Catholic on the one side, Protestant on the
other. What was I going to do with the white heritage in the family which is
deep and pervasive? I wasn't going to walk away from it and not deal with it
as certain writers, whom I won't mention. I wanted to take that on. I wanted
to just take on the complexity of black life, and I didn't see any writers doing
that much of it. I knew I had a lot to write about. To find the form—that
was the question.

**Rowell:** You were in a very peculiar circumstance. On the one hand, white
publishers were not welcoming black writers, and, on the other, being surrounded by advocates of the Black Arts Movement, who were not really interested in the kind of work you do, you were not really embraced by the black
literary establishment either.
**Forrest:** Toni Morrison, Toni Morrison, Toni Morrison to the rescue!

**Rowell:** You must have been a black writer in search of a place and in search
of black writers or black editors who could nourish you.
**Forrest:** That's right. See and that's why I can't put down the integration/
Black Power Movement too much because that vaulted Toni Morrison into
a position there at Random House. She was hired, promoted there, because
they knew that there was an audience out there with all this energy. "Well,
we need a black person in here to publish some of this. It probably won't
last long"—I think that was their thinking—"but let's see what we can do
and get it known." One of my editors at *Muhammad Speaks,* who had a connection in New York, passed on my manuscript to another editor, then

at Holt. And he said he liked it, but it just didn't seem to hold together and he said, "Well, you know, we recently published a novel by a new black writer, Toni Morrison. I don't know if you've heard of her or not, but a novel called *The Bluest Eye*. It happened that one of my secretaries at *Muhammad Speaks* had a copy of *The Bluest Eye*, and she was reading it and she said, "You know, Mr. Forrest, I know you like to read novels. Why don't you take this book." So she gave it to me. Of course, the book now is worth about a thousand dollars. And subsequently, I called Morrison and got to her after three rings. Because she was just developing—she had just been promoted—she was developing a stable of writers. And I told her—at the time I did have a little background since I was associate editor of *Muhammad Speaks*—a little bit about myself and so on. And she said, "Well, why don't you send me that manuscript?" You know all these things are unheard of today. I did so, on one weekend, say on like a Thursday. Probably the next Friday of the next week I got a call from her, and she was just elated over it. This was a lot of the material that went into *There Is a Tree*. In a sense, I was able to vault over both the narrows of the Black Aesthetic and the narrows of the White Aesthetic, because of the new energies created in the society by the Civil Rights Movement, by the Black Power Movement, by some interest in getting some new energies into American literature. And it seemed as if maybe that was happening in black life. Morrison was absolutely an angel for me, because, as you know, her interest in serious literature, her interest in language, character—these are all things that I'm interested in. We hit it off quite well, and I was extremely lucky to have my manuscript placed in her hands.

On one of my trips there to New York—because I was the editor of *Muhammad Speaks* and had written something about *Invisible Man* and gotten in touch with Ellison, he said he was very interested in having me interview him. I had the bound galleys to *There Is a Tree*, when I went to interview him. It almost seemed that I had been out in the wilderness all these years, and then suddenly things came together for me. But I don't ever downgrade—I don't mean to downgrade for a minute—the energies that were broken open by the political forces, even some that I don't necessarily agree with in the society, because that forced the establishment to look to a middle ground, and that's where my work is. It's black and it's evolved in classical connection. The other question was how many people were writing novels at the time? Well, not that many. And not that many blacks. That happens later, in the later 1970s and 1980s. All of these things came together.

**Rowell:** Those years, when you worked as a journalist, were obviously important for the making of your first novel as well as for the Leon Forrest we know now.

**Forrest:** Oh, sure that's right, because I had the advantage of working at papers where I could get out a certain type of heat and protest and anger, and I could come home to write at night and think more in terms as a fiction writer. So that was a benefit. Then there was a benefit of just learning how to write a good sentence or a good paragraph at a paper. One of my chores at *Muhammad Speaks* was to put the whole paper together each week, and organize it. And when I got that assignment from the editor, I said, "Oh, my god, I can't do this because I have very little mechanical ability"—but I learned that and learned how to do it rather well. I found that organizing principle also helps with my own writing and fiction. How am I going to put this story together? How am I going to put this paper to bed? All these things were a benefit to me that I've used over the years. Also to be around the Muslims, and yet not be a Muslim. I've written about Muslims in my novels as well. All of this is so exciting for a young writer to have that kind of influence, and you're absolutely right about your vision of the barbershop—to go back to your point that the barbershop is a kind of university—that university is in the barbershop, it's in the university, it's in the streets, it's in church, it's in nursing homes it's everywhere that you can find a range of human voices and some index into human joy and suffering.

**Rowell:** There is a long distance from your work as a journalist and your first novel, *There Is a Tree*. There is a long distance and yet there are also only one or two steps, probably at the same time; from that novel and that journalistic experience to *Divine Days*. Will you talk about the geneology of the making of *Divine Days*?

**Forrest:** One of the things that's hard to tell students in writing class in that a writer—if he or she is going to be anything—must almost be insanely ambitious. And hope to God that he or she finds an outlet for that. I shouldn't just say writers—you'd say that with musicians and so on. You notice how the tension of this creativity and self-destruction has killed people like Parker who was attempting to go all the way with his music, or with Coltrane maybe even more. So I am blessed by having found a form, finally, to shape out all of this yeast, this materiality, this heartbreak and joy and hilarity that seems to be always bubbling up in my consciousness. Also I started *Divine Days* at a time in my life—I was 47, I guess—when I guess I should say I was coming into the

height of my creative powers. I finished it when I was 55. I worked on it for
about seven years. And I was able to, I think, bring into some sort of relief,
stark relief, all the reading I had been doing in the university. Reading is enormously important to a writer, and being able to turn that reading right back
into what you're writing. So I was reading, and reading everything I could get
my hands on in the classes I was teaching and things that I was doing. And
then I finally had received enough detachment in time to deal with the life I
had in bars, where I worked as a bartender for many years. It suddenly
occurred to me one day, "You know you had all these different interesting people you knew. Why don't you see what you can do with them?" Charles, what I
did one summer was to sit out in the park and tape memories of the bar, characters and so on. Then I would go to the typewriter and either just straight type
down what I had put on the tape recorder, or in many cases, transform it even
as I was listening to it. In the transforming of it, I was finally able to take some
of those character shapings of people I had known and turn them into something quite different from, though connected with, the people I had known in
bars. But I'm talking about, perhaps, twenty years after the fact. By now, I could
see these things in terms of my own powers of the imagination to transform. I
had the confidence. I thought I had the language, and I had enough of the
memory of these things to have a semblance of the way people talk, and yet
also enough confidence to transform them into coinages of my own creation.

The other thing was of course, the expansive connection with close reading of *Ulysses* and jazz, and trying to see how I could broaden the structure of
my novels. I was very interested now in trying to create sustained character
development, an interest in mind in the *Bloodworth Orphans*. But now I
thought I had the maturity to do this. Of course, you need that kind of maturity to be able to put your major characters in a variety of waters, a variety of
troubles, a variety of situations. And then out of that they come away with
new layers of consciousness revealed to us. That was another development or
evolution with *Divine Days*. Another thing that happened was that, as I was
writing, jokes would come popping up to me, ideas, storylines, vignettes, that
I had forgotten about—"Oh, don't forget that. Oh, stick that in." And so it
was probably the most fun of any novel I've ever written. That was good,
given the length of it and also the comic force that is in and out of the other
novels. But it seems to have been an almost volcanic power in me in this
particular novel, in *Divine Days*. All of these things coming together at a
certain time in my development are part of the creation of what went into
*Divine Days*.

# Index